The Handbook of
GAMES & PASTIMES

Edited by
KENNETH WHEELER

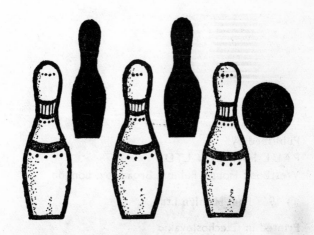

PAUL HAMLYN · LONDON

Published by
PAUL HAMLYN LTD
Westbook House, Fulham Broadway, London

© 1963 Paul Hamlyn Ltd

Printed in Czechoslovakia

T 1229

CONTENTS

INTRODUCTION

Recreation is a necessary part of everyone's life, and games of skill and chance have been played since the beginning of history.

This book is not concerned with the athletic sports and team games which are nowadays organised for spectators as well as players, but it deals with popular indoor and outdoor pastimes for children and adults which require none but the simplest equipment.

In the following pages you will discover hundreds of ways to spend a quiet hour by the fireside, diversions while travelling, and exciting games for parties, for the beach and for the garden.

Careful preparation beforehand is the main secret of success for a party, whether for children or grown-ups. Plan ahead in detail, make sure that you have all the equipment that you need ready at hand, and when your guests arrive you can concentrate your attention on them and share their enjoyment.

Make sure that you know the rules of the games you intend to play so that you can explain them simply and then exercise unobtrusive control over the activity as it proceeds. All games need some discipline for full enjoyment, especially when children are concerned, but this should be applied with subtlety. Party-fun which appears spontaneous is usually always carefully organised beforehand.

Don't keep a game going too long—change to another activity long before the fun starts to flag.

For very young children the recipe is (a) toys to play with amongst themselves; (b) a few simple mass-activities with small, but imaginative prizes for everyone; (c) jelly, ice cream and pop for tea; (d) balloons; (e) a surprise gift to take home.

For older children, pencil and paper games can be introduced during quieter moments. Shyness can be overcome by games which require the formation of teams and partnerships. Generally speaking, no teen-age party is complete without some form of music and dancing.

For adults you must be careful to suit the particular personalities of your guests, but most people enjoy being crazy once in a while, so you could include a few children's games in your programme with hilarious results.

Parties for special occasions need more planning and attention to atmosphere.

An index to the games described in this book has been added for easy reference.

CHILDREN'S PARTY GAMES

There are no hard-and-fast rules for preparing parties, but the following comments will give a general guide.

Children's parties are usually given to celebrate a birthday. For the 2 year-old this will be the first realisation of the meaning of the event, so a simple present, and a decorated sponge cake, bearing two candles, are all that are required to ensure a happy occasion.

From the age of 3, however, parties take on a meaning. Having decided Johnny or Jenny shall have a party, 'Who shall be invited?' may well be the main question to decide. Whatever the age of the young host or hostess, guests should essentially be friends—indeed he or she should play the main part in deciding who should be present.

An important point to bear in mind is that, wherever possible, children should be of the same age. It is quite impossible to entertain satisfactorily on the same level a group of children whose ages range from 3 to 15 years old. If, however, a mixed age group cannot be avoided, concentrate on competitive games, i.e. games where the children participate individually, as in games of hide-and-seek, and in pencil and paper games. The attention of the older children can be engaged by allowing them to be judges.

How many guests should be invited? The total should be limited according to the age of your child. For a 3 year-old four or five friends are sufficient, and seven or eight friends for the 4 year-old. At 5 years, with the experience of school atmosphere, up to twelve friends could be accepted. Beyond this age, up to 10 years old, twenty guests is probably the maximum that can comfortably be handled.

When making out the invitations, it is wise to state a time at which the children are to be 'collected' by their parents, and this should not be too late. This applies particularly to the younger children as they tire more quickly. In general $2\frac{1}{2}$–3 hours is a sufficient period of time for a children's party. The maxim, 'Enough is as good as a feast' is a prudent guide. It is far better for a guest to leave regretfully, than to be keen to depart. Any visitor wishing to remain is satisfaction and reward in itself for all your efforts.

Entertainment of your guests requires some thought and organisation, and what to include in the programme depends mainly on the age group to be entertained. Children under 5 years old, although happy to be amongst other children, are not sufficiently advanced physically, mentally and socially to take in the group games where interplay is required. For this group, a few toys will provide quite sufficient amusement, and the party tea can be the highlight. A suitable time for tea would be 4.30 p.m., guests having arrived half an hour or one hour previously. Allow a little time for play after tea, then farewells can start at 5.30 p.m.

For the older children, games are required ranging from the simplest, i.e. nursery rhymes, to the more developed games, according to age. In general, allow the group of children as large a space as possible! Four children can utilise far more space than four adults.

Plan a full programme, but don't adhere to it rigidly; be pliable. Usually the children will themselves suggest the games they like best and want to play. This should be encouraged.

Older children have a sense of organisation, and will be happiest playing games of their choice. However, long before a game can become monotonous and interest palls, change to some other. Keep their interest throughout. Children quickly become bored and from this riotous conduct can result.

Where a number of boys are together, some noise and roughness is inevitable. This is where the services of a jolly 'Uncle' will be useful. A grown-up who is willing to join in a rough and tumble with the little rascals will help to keep rowdiness in bounds.

At the other extreme, there may be one or two children at the party who, for some reason or other, fail to mix with the others and do not wish to join in the games. In such a situation don't be over-insistent that the child should mix, but simply give him a book or a toy to play with until he wishes to join in voluntarily.

Sometimes, too, there may be a child who is inclined to be self-assertive. Direction into a rôle of responsibility, or casting as the leader in a game, is often the best method of dealing with this type of child.

Children all enjoy party hats, crackers and balloons. Provide at least two balloons per person so that there are sufficient for games and replace-ments, perhaps also allowing for a third to be taken away at the end of the party.

Each child should receive a small gift or prize in the form of a few sweets or small book or toy. Be cunning in the distribution of prizes to the younger ones, so that a prize is received by each (even if this means a little cheating on your part). Alternatively, the gifts can be put in a bran tub and each child allowed to dip for a small treasure before leaving for home. For the older children, prizes can of course be awarded on a competitive basis.

The actual tea is an important feature, but your catering need not be elaborate. In fact, the simpler the better. With young children especially, 'new' dishes are risky. For the 3–5 year-olds, serve simple sandwiches, plain buns colourfully iced, assorted biscuits, ice cream and jelly, and the birthday cake with milk or fruit juice to drink. For the older children, the sandwiches can be more varied and savouries such as sausage rolls can be included. Chocolate biscuits, buns and cake may be served in addition to jelly, ice cream and birthday cake, with tea and fizzy drinks.

It is best to avoid very sickly cakes with cream, especially if it is at a time of year when children are generally attending a number of parties, for too much can prove upsetting. After tea have the children sing nursery rhymes or songs. This, too, will help prevent possible digestive disturbances.

It is well, too, to bear in mind that with a number of children some accidents, such as breakage of crockery, spilling of drinks, and so on are inevitable. Preparation for possible misfortune will help you to accept and deal with it the more calmly.

Be quite relaxed and you will enjoy the party as much as the children do.

MUSICAL GAMES (2—5 YEARS)

Ring a Ring o' Roses

Children make a circle moving round whilst the following is sung:

> Ring a ring o' roses,
> A pocketful of posies,
> Atishoo! Atishoo!
> All fall down.

'Atishoo' is mimed, and as the last line is sung the children fall gently to the floor.

Oranges and Lemons

This is a group musical action game to the tune 'Oranges and Lemons'. Two of the children form an arch by facing each other and holding hands, arms outstretched. One child elects to be 'Orange', the other 'Lemon'. The remaining children pass through the arch again and again in a circular direction whilst the following is sung:

'Oranges and lemons,' say the bells of St Clement's,
'You owe me five farthings,' say the bells of St Martin's.
'When will you pay me?' say the bells of Old Bailey,
'When I grow rich,' say the bells of Shoreditch.
'When will that be?' say the bells of Stepney,
'I am sure I don't know,' says the great bell of Bow.
Here comes a candle to light you to bed,
Here comes a chopper to chop off your head,
Chip! chop! chip! chop!

While singing the last line, the children forming the arch move their arms up and down in a chopper-like action finally catching one of the children passing through the arch. The victim is then asked to select 'Orange' or 'Lemon'. Having made the choice, e.g. 'Lemon', the victim then takes a position behind the child forming the arch who elected to be 'Lemon'.

This procedure continues until all the children are behind the two forming the arch when a 'tug of war' takes place to decide whether 'Oranges' or 'Lemons' are victors.

Miming Nursery Rhymes

All the commonly known Nursery Rhymes are suitable; e.g. 'Pussy Cat, Pussy Cat where have you been?' 'Ding Dong Bell', 'Georgie Porgie', 'Little Miss Muffet'.

Method: The rhyme is recited or sung and appropriate actions performed.

Example: Pat-a-cake, pat-a-cake, baker's man,
　　　　(Imaginary cake patted)
　　Bake me a cake as quick as you can,
　　　　(Gestures of agitation)
　　Pat it and prick it and mark it with 'B',
　　　　(Mimed)
　　Put it in the oven for baby and me.
　　　　(Imaginary opening of oven door and indication to Baby and self)

Farmer in the Den

A musical game with action. One child impersonates the 'Farmer', the remaining children form a circle around him. The following is sung whilst circling round the farmer:

　　　　The Farmer in his den,
　　　　The Farmer in his den,
　　　　Heigh-ho, heigh-ho,
　　　　The Farmer in his den.

　　　　The Farmer wants a wife,
　　　　The Farmer wants a wife,
　　　　Heigh-ho, heigh-ho,
　　　　The Farmer wants a wife.

(Here the Farmer chooses a 'wife' to stand in the circle with him).

> *The wife wants a child,*
> *The wife wants a child,*
> *Heigh-ho, heigh-ho,*
> *The wife wants a child.*

(The Farmer's wife now chooses her 'child' to stand in the middle).

> *The child wants a nurse,*
> *The child wants a nurse,*
> *Heigh-ho, heigh-ho,*
> *The child wants a nurse.*

(A 'nurse' is now chosen by the 'child' and stands in the centre).

> *The nurse wants a dog,*
> *The nurse wants a dog,*
> *Heigh-ho, heigh-ho,*
> *The nurse wants a dog.*

(A 'dog' takes his place in the centre, chosen by the 'nurse').

> *We all pat the dog,*
> *We all pat the dog,*
> *Heigh-ho, heigh-ho,*
> *We all pat the dog.*

After each verse, a child is chosen and stands within the circle. With the last verse however, the 'dog' is patted as the appropriate words are sung. The 'dog' becomes 'Farmer' and the game recommences.

The Mulberry Bush

A game in which the children walk round in a circle, miming the following song:

(*Verse One*)
  Here we go round the mulberry bush,
  The mulberry bush, the mulberry bush,
  Herre we go round the mulberry bush,
  On a cold and frosty morning.
(*Verse Two*)
  This is the way we warm our hands,
  Warm our hands, warm our hands,
  This is the way we warm our hands,
  On a cold and frosty morning.
      (The hands are rubbed together)

The following may also be sung with suitable actions performed.

  This is the way we warm our feet
    (Running on spot)
  This is the way be brush our teeth,
  This is the way we comb our hair,
  This is the way we run to school,
  This is the way we write in school, etc.

Looby Loo

A musical game with actions performed as the words are sung. A circle is made and the children skip round singing the following:
            Here we go (or dance) looby loo,
            Here we go looby light,
            Here we go looby loo,
            All on a Saturday night.

> *Put all your right hands in*
> *And shake them all around,*
> *Take all your right hands out*
> *And turn yourselves about.*

(Do the same with the left hand as well, then both hands).

> *Put all your right feet in*
> *And shake them all around,*
> *Take all your right feet out*
> *And turn yourselves about.*

(Repeat this verse saying 'left foot in').

> *Put your both feet in*
> *And shake them all around*
> *Take your both feet out,*
> *And turn yourselves about.*

(Finish the game by singing).

> *Put your whole self in*
> *And shake yourself about,*
> *Take your whole self out*
> *And turn yourselves about.*

What Time is it, Mr Wolf?

An active game, not musical.

The children follow one child, who is Mr Wolf, demanding again and again: 'What time is it Mr Wolf?' Mr Wolf replies by giving the time of his choice, but immediately he says 'Dinner time' the children run away beyond a pre-set line. Any child tagged before reaching the safety area becomes 'Mr Wolf' for the next game.

Three Blind Mice

A well known nursery rhyme which is sung, with appropriate actions.

A 'Farmer's Wife' is chosen and the remaining children form a circle round her. They then move around singing:

> *Three blind mice, three blind mice,*
> *See how they run, see how they run,*
> *They all run after the Farmer's wife,*
> *Who cut off their tails with a carving knife,*
> *Did you ever see such a thing in your life as*
> *Three blind mice·*

The 'Farmer's Wife' menacingly brandishes an imaginary knife, the circle breaks and the children run away. The object is then for the 'Farmer's Wife' to tag a child, who then becomes the 'wife' for the next game.

MUSICAL GAMES (5—12 YEARS)

Junior Paul Jones

A 'starter' or 'introducing' game. Girls form a circle and move in a clockwise direction. Boys make a circle, being on the outside, and walk round anti-clockwise. Music is played, and when it stops each boy and girl found facing each other must perform any action demanded of them.

Examples: Ask your partner's name,
Ask which school he or she attends,
Shake hands and bow/curtsy, respectively,

Join crossed hands and take five steps to the left, seven to the right,
Discover the colour of your partner's eyes, etc.

Owls

Groups of three are formed, the two outer children of a group clasping hands with each other around the middle child. One single child standing between the groups is an 'owl' without a 'tree'. When the music stops playing, the 'owls' are released to find another 'tree' group, the extra child joining in the hunt. The child subsequently left without a 'tree' then stands alone amidst the groups and the game starts again.

Musical Crosses

Crosses (chalked, taped or crossed strips of cardboard) are placed at intervals about the floor, one less than the number of players taking part. The children make a circle around the room, outside the crosses, and walk round to music. The music stops and each child must then stand on a cross. As the music restarts the one child unplaced stands on a cross. This is repeated until all but one of the crosses is occupied, then the last round takes place. The winner is the child obtaining a place on the remaining cross.

Nursery Rhyme Relay

A singing game for two groups. Two teams are formed, and one starts to sing a nursery rhyme. As soon as the first rhyme has been sung, the second team replies by singing another rhyme. This is continued until one side is unable to produce a different rhyme and so is defeated.

Musical Pairs

Two children form an arch and the remaining pairs of children walk under the arch to music. When the music ceases any pair found under the arch are 'caught'. They then form an arch themselves at some distance from the original arch. The game continues until only one pair remains uncaught, and that pair is the winner.

Musical Elimination

Children form a circle and pass around an object, e.g. ball or small box. Anyone caught holding the object when the music stops is eliminated, and the game proceeds until only one player—the winner—remains.

BALLOON GAMES

Blow Balloon Relay

Required for this game: one balloon, and one drinking straw per person. A space of approximately five yards is marked at each boundary, by a chalk line or with a piece of string.

Two teams of equal numbers are formed. The balloon is blown from the starting line to the far line, and back, by each member of the team in relays. All blowing is done through a drinking straw. The first team to finish is the winner.

Balloon Handball

Two rows of chairs are placed, facing each other,

approximately 4 ft. apart. The teams take their seats and aim to tap the balloon over and behind their opponents. Scoring: If the balloon touches the ground behind a team, a point is awarded to the opposing side. Should a player rise from his seat, a penalty may be awarded in the form of a ½ point deduction.

Rules: Hands only (open) must be used.

Players must remain seated.

Mid-air Balloon

A game for small groups or teams. Each group has one balloon and aims to keep its balloon in the air by blowing. Hands may not be used. Each time the balloon is touched, or falls to the ground, a point is scored against the team concerned. After a set period of time, the team with least points against it is the winner.

Balloon Passing Race

Two or more teams are formed. Each team forms a 'queue' and its members stand with feet apart. The balloon is passed through the legs to the back of the team. The last player, or 'anchor-man', runs to the front of the team and the action is repeated until the players have restored themselves to their original team places. The first team to complete the relay action is the winner.

Back-pass Balloon Race

Group of equal numbers form circles. The leader of each group commences the race—the balloon being passed behind the back from player to player. A circuit should be completed a given number of times. If the balloon is dropped, the circuit must be recommenced.

Push Balloon Relay

A game for two or more teams, requiring one folded newspaper and one sausage-shaped balloon per team. Two parallel lines are marked approximately 12 ft. apart to denote starting and finishing respectively. Each team starts by pushing the balloon, at its end only, with the newspaper, reaching the far line and then returning. The second player does likewise and so on; the first team completing the course is the winner.

TAG GAMES

Hill Dill

The room in which the game is to be played is divided into three areas, e.g. by chalk lines. Two equal groups of children stand in the two outer areas, while one single player stands in the central section. This child calls out 'Hill Dill, come over the Hill'. At this command, groups must change over to the opposite area. Meantime, the centre child tags as many players as possible as they cross over. Those tagged remain in the centre to tag more next time as they attempt to recross. The winner is the one child who remains untagged at the end.

French Tag

The object of this game is to tag a player in an awkward spot, e.g. ankle or knee. When tagged, the player must chase the others, holding that area of the body which has been touched.

Chain Tag

Two players commence the game, joining hands. Each subsequent player who is tagged must join up to become part of the chain until all but the winner have been caught.

Deportment Tag

The basic game of tag is played, but this time with everyone balancing an object on the head, e.g. a domino, or small book. Touching the object with the hand is not permitted.

Ball Tag

A large ball is required. This is passed from child to child as the players stand in a circle. One player runs round the outside of the circle, attempting to tag the ball as it is passed. The child found holding the ball when it is successfully tagged must change places with the chaser.

Cat and Mouse

All the children, except two, form two lines and join hands. One of the two children left out is named 'cat', the other 'mouse'. The former proceeds to chase the mouse up and down between the lines, the direction of which is changed at a given signal. For example, at a blow of a whistle, or at a call from the leader, the children make a half turn, rejoin hands, and make lines in another direction.

Human Noughts and Crosses

Nine chairs are required, and these are placed in rows of three.

Two teams of six or more children are given numbers. When a number is called the appropriate 'number' from each team takes a seat of his choice. The first team to have three of its players seated in a straight or diagonal row is the winner of that game.

GAMES OF THROWING

Matchbox Skittles

Required: six matchboxes and one tennis ball.

The matchboxes represent skittles and are placed in a line, at distances of approximately 4 in. apart. The player takes his or her place behind a set line, at least 10 ft. from the skittles, then rolls the tennis ball in an attempt to knock down as many matchboxes as possible. The winner is the one to knock down the greatest number of skittles in one or more attempts, or the first player to obtain a pre-set target score.

In the Vessel

Four sets of ten playing cards, each of a different suit, and a bucket or large bowl are required. Four players, each with his own suit of cards (i.e. hearts, spades, diamonds, clubs) attempt to flick the cards into the bucket from a distance of at least 10 ft. (To flick a card it is held horizontally between the first and second fingers). The winner is the one who succeeds in getting most cards in the vessel.

This can easily be adapted to make a team game.

Plate Collection

A metal or enamel plate is required. This is placed on the floor 6 ft. to 9 ft. from the players. Playing cards, counters, pennies or other coins are aimed on to the plate by each player in turn. Players should be allotted a set number of throws, and the competitor getting the most objects to remain on the plate is the winner. Alternatively, this can be a 'free for all' with a time limit imposed.

Mock Basket Ball

This game requires to be played on a smooth surface, so a carpeted floor is not suitable.

Required: one ping-pong ball, one basket (an ordinary shopping basket with handle adds to the fun).

The basket is placed on the floor. This is the goal into which the ping-pong ball is to be thrown or bounced from a distance of approximately 7 ft. Ten attempts are allowed, and the player with the highest score is the winner. One point is awarded each time the ball remains in the basket—no score if the ball bounces out again.

Basin Ball

This is a variation of Mock Basket Ball and played similarly. The difference is that a basin is used instead of a basket and the difficulty is not so much getting the ball in the basin, as getting it to remain there. An accurate, but not too forceful bounce usually does the trick.

Roll or Bowl a Penny

Requirements for this game are pennies, and a tumbler or similar receptacle, e.g. small bucket or basin. The object of the game is to score by getting the pennies to remain in the receptacle which lies on its side, a bowling or rolling action being used. The player 'bowls' from a distance of approximately 10 ft. and the winner is the one with the highest score, either within a pre-set time, or after a given number of attempts.

Cover the Target

This may be an individual or team game. The target is a small coin placed on the floor about 12 in. from a wall. From a distance of 10 ft. the player rolls larger coins, aiming to cover the target. The first to succeed within a given period is the winner. It does not count, however, if the coin covers the target by rebounding from the wall.

Miniature Bowls (for two or more players)

Allow each player four small balls (e.g. ping-pong or golf) and one extra which is the 'Jack'. Each player should have balls with a certain distinguishing mark. The 'Jack' should have a marking distinctive from all others.

The area required is 12 sq. ft. or thereabouts, and the 'Jack' is placed in the area and to one side. The player bowls from a point on the boundary parallel to the 'Jack' and rolls each of his four balls towards the 'Jack', the object being to get one ball as near to it as possible. Then his opponent rolls and tries to replace the ball nearest the 'Jack' with one of his own.

Scoring: one point is allowed to the player whose ball is nearest the 'Jack' at the conclusion of an 'end'. The winner is the first one to obtain a set number of points, or alternatively the one who, after a set number of 'ends', can show the highest score.

RACES

Potato Race

For each team, or individual competitor, a suitable receptacle is required, e.g. a cardboard box or stiff paper bag. Four or five potatoes per team or single competitor are also required. The receptacle is placed on a line, behind which the children stand. A first row of potatoes is placed 5 or 6 yards from the starting line and other rows are set up at intervals of 3–4 ft. along the course. A starting signal is given. The players have to race toward the first row of potatoes, pick one up, and race back to the starting line, putting the potatoes in the receptacle. This continues until one competitor has collected all his quota. He then either signals by raising both hands above his head, or takes the bag of potatoes to a designated winning point.

Double Bend

This may be organised as a straightforward race, divided into heats, or as a team relay race. The hazard of the race is that each competitor is required to grasp his own ankles, and maintain this position, while covering the 'course' that has been set at the fastest possible speed.

Fan the Kipper Relay

Required: one newspaper, folded fanwise, and a 'kipper' (fish-shape cut from a piece of tissue paper approximately 10 in. × 4 in.) per team. The method is for each player to 'fan the kipper' over a set course, propelling the kipper by waving the paper fan behind it to create a helpful draught of air. This race is continued in relay fashion, the first team home being the victor.

Paper Bag Relay

A relay race for two competing teams of equal number. Each competitor must be provided with a paper bag of a standard size. The teams form up facing each other at a distance apart of approximately 7 ft. Each player, in relay order, runs round his own team at the same time blowing up the bag he carries. Then, on returning to his place, he must burst the bag between his hands before the next runner is permitted to start his circuit. The first team to finish, with all bags burst, is the winner.

How Many Feathers?

Another relay race requiring four down-feathers, and a piece of cardboard approximately 5 sq. in. for each person.

The players are divided into teams of equal number, each team appointing its own leader who is provided with a pencil and paper. The leaders take up position at one end of the room, each facing his own team which is lined up at the opposite end.

At a starting signal, each player must walk to his leader, holding before him all the time the cardboard on which four feathers have been placed. The leader jots down the number of feathers remaining on the cardboard of each team member as he reaches him. After all the contestants have taken a turn, leaders total their scores. The team losing the least feathers, wins.

Ducks to Water

The children are divided into groups of six or seven. Both groups then form lines, each person in the knees-bend position, placing his or her hands on the shoulders of the one in front. In this position, each group proceeds to walk to a set goal, e.g. a chalked circle at the opposite side of the room. The leader giving the starting signal may also keep competitors in step by calling: 'left-right'. The first group to reach its goal without breaking formation is the winner.

Tiddlywink Race

This may be played in relay formation, in which case each team requires one container (e.g. egg-cup) and one large and one small tiddlywink. The egg-cup container is placed approximately 12 ft. from the starting line, and each player must aim to get the small tiddlywink into the egg-cup by flicking with the larger one. On doing so, he returns the tiddlywinks to the starting line and hands them over to the next player in his team who at once sets about the same task.

O'Grady Says...

Physical jerks with a difference! For this game a leader is elected, who is 'O'Grady'. The others stand before him, adequately spaced. The leader gives orders such as 'O'Grady says hands on head; O'Grady says knees bend', etc., and all must obey. However, if the command only is given without the prefix 'O'Grady says', that particular order must be ignored, and the previous one continued. Competitors who break these rules are at once eliminated, until one only remains, who is the winner.

Examples: O'Grady says 'Clap hands' – 'Arms stretch forward' – 'About turn' – 'Touch the toes' – 'Run on the spot' – 'Sideways bend to right' – 'Sideways bend to left' – 'Touch left shoulder with right hand' – 'Touch right shoulder with left hand' – 'Arms stretch above head'.

SEEKING GAMES

All Change

The players sit in a circle, in the centre of which is a blindfolded child. The circle of players are each given the name of a city or country. A leader calls out two or more of the names, and those called are required to change places with each other. The object for the blindfolded child is to try to catch a player while places are being changed. To give a fair chance to the centre player, names of those seated opposite each other should be called, and if the blindfolded player has difficulty in making a 'catch', 'All change' should be called. At this command, all the circle players must change to the place directly opposite them.

Squeak, Piggy, Squeak

A popular game, particularly with the younger members of this age group.

One player, who is blindfolded and equipped with a cushion, stands in the centre of a circle formed by the others, who sit on chairs or cross-legged on the floor. The one blindfolded is guided around the inside of the circle until he says 'stop', when he is placed in position facing the nearest player. He then proceeds to place the cushion on the knees of the seated player, sits upon it and says 'Squeak, Piggy, Squeak'. This player must squeak in response, whereupon the blindfolded child has to guess the owner of the voice. If a correct guess is made, places are changed, otherwise the procedure is repeated.

Blind Man

In this game, all the players seek a hidden object, which the host should place in a spot where it may be found without having to move any other article in the process. As each player spots the object, without giving any indication of having done so, he should quietly sit down. The last player to be seated is the 'blind man'.

Blind Man's Buff

One person is blindfolded, the remainder move around freely. The players have to avoid the 'blind man', while his object is to try to touch someone. Whenever a successful 'touch' is made, places are changed.

Have you Seen the Muffin Man?

In principle, this game is similar to 'Squeak, Piggy, Squeak', and equally popular with the younger children.

One player stands blindfolded in the centre of a circle. The children forming the circle move round singing:

Have you seen the muffin man, the muffin man,
the muffin man,
Have you seen the muffin man who lives in Drury Lane?

The blindfolded player then points at random and the nearest player in that direction steps forward. The 'muffin man' may then ask three questions requiring brief replies. e.g. 'Do you like to go to school?' Or, 'Do you like pink ice-cream?' Three guesses to try to name the player who answered are then allowed, and if the guess is correct the circle player takes his place as the 'muffin man'. If the guess is incorrect the same player retains the role of 'muffin man' until he succeeds in identifying a victim.

Hunt the Thimble

Any small object may be used, although a thimble is traditional and has given the game its title.

The player elected 'seeker' leaves the room, during which time the object is hidden. The seeker then comes back and attempts to find the object.

Spectators help by giving clues. They cry 'cold' when the searcher is far from the object, 'freezing' when he is very far away, 'hot' when he is close to the place and 'boiling' when very near, and so on. Alternatively, music may be used to indicate to the seeker his relative distance from the object, e.g. softest when far away, becoming louder as the seeker gets near hiding place. However, children usually enjoy taking part in giving clues.

QUIET GAMES

Oral Games

Reflection

A leader makes various statements, such as 'I combed my hair'. 'I went to the fair'. 'I clapped my hands'. To each of these remarks, the remainder are instructed to reply: 'Just like me'. Unknown to the players, the last statement of all will be: 'And there I saw a Monkey', to which the reply will follow automatically!

Acting Nursery Rhymes

Two teams or groups are formed, one of which selects a nursery rhyme which it proceeds to act. The second group has to guess the rhyme being acted, then selects and acts its own rhyme. Mime may be used if desired.

Lock and Key

A game with a similar snare. The leader makes statements like these:

> '*I am an aluminium lock*',
> '*I am a silver lock*',
> '*I am an iron lock*', *etc.*

To each of these remarks, the remainder reply, substituting 'key' for lock. 'I am an aluminium *key*', etc. The final statement, however, is: 'I am a monk lock'. To which the reply will be 'I am a monk—key'!!

Spelling Bee Elimination

This may be a straight-forward spelling contest between two teams, words being selected to suit the ages of the players. A word is given to each team member in turn. If incorrectly spelt, he or she is eliminated and the same word given to the next player, and so on through the team until correctly spelt. The game continues until one team is entirely eliminated.

Rhyme Elimination

A quiet game which can be played seated. One child begins by saying: 'I want a rhyme in next to no time and the word I choose is...' Each child in turn gives a word rhyming with the one selected. If for instance 'bat' is chosen, replies could be 'rat, mat, gnat, etc.' Should a player be stuck for an answer, he or she is eliminated and the next player restarts the game. The last player remaining is the winner.

I Spy

A favourite game with the younger children.

One child selects an object in the room and states: 'I spy with my little eye, something beginning with..........' and here gives the initial letter of the object of his choice, e.g. 'C' for chair, or 'S' for sweets. The remaining children are allowed to make one guess each, in turn, until the article has been named. The child giving the correct answer becomes the next player to 'spy'.

Pencil and Paper Games

Pairs

Here is a simple 'rest' game to play between energetic activities.

The first article of a pair is given, the children being required to write down its partner. After, say, 20 questions have been posed, those players with highest scores may be awarded a small prize. Examples of pairs: Hat and Coat – Knife and Fork – Mother and Father – Cup and Saucer – Pen and Ink – Cat and Dog – Shoes and Socks – Brother and Sister – Boy and Girl – Hands and Feet – Peaches and Cream – Curds and Whey – Yours and Mine – Gold and Silver – Men and Women – Horse and Cart – Bacon and Egg – Cowboys and Indians – King and Queen – Brush and Comb.

Alternatively, questions may be formed as follows: 'What goes with Fork? What goes with Hat?' etc.

Handicap Drawing

Players are asked to draw a simple object, e.g. Cat, Tree, House, *but with the hand not normally used*. This is often great fun, for some children (and grown-ups) find themselves practically helpless with their 'wrong' hand. Prizes can be awarded to those making the best efforts.

Photographic Observation

Show the players a number of photographs or drawings of various objects. These could be cut from a magazine and attached to a large sheet of stiff paper prior to the party. Use definite objects, e.g. a pipe, motor car, washing machine, television set, etc. Show all the pictures for approximately five minutes, then remove them. The players make a list of all the articles they have seen, the winner being the one submitting the longest correct list of objects.

Hangman

This is a popular game, well known to most children.

The game may be played by two or more players. The leader draws a hangman's gallows on a piece of paper or a blackboard. He selects a word and draws a dotted line, each dot representing one letter of the word. Each person in turn now has the opportunity of guessing one letter in the word by asking 'Is there an "I" in it?', or whatever other letter he chooses. If the word does contain an 'I', this is placed in the word at the appropriate dot:

if not, part of the hanged man is drawn, first the head, then the trunk, then the limbs. Other features may be added if desired. A child who succeeds in completing a word before the man is hanged may be allowed to lead the next game.

Community Drawing

The children sit in groups of four or five, each player armed with a strip of paper and pencil. Number one in each group draws a man's head, then folds the top of the paper over his drawing and passes the slip on to the next child in his group. Number two then adds shoulders and arms, folds the paper and passes it to the next child as before. The drawing continues, with further parts of the body being added unseen. Numbers four or five may then be asked to give the drawing an appropriate name, after which the whole is revealed. Though not normally competitive, this game can be most amusing.

SIMPLE CARD GAMES

Snap

A well-known card game which is a particular favourite with young children. Two or more players can take part. Allow one pack of ordinary playing cards per six players. And an umpire with sharp ears is a decided asset!

The cards are all dealt out and the player keeps them before him, face down. Each player in turn then takes the top card placing it face upwards before him. As soon as any two identical cards can be spotted anywhere on the table (i.e. two sixes, two tens, two Kings, etc.), 'Snap' is called. The first to call 'Snap' adds to the bottom of his own pack all the cards of the pile(s) on top of which the identical cards appeared. When each player has turned up all his or her cards, they are turned over and played again. The game continues, with players dropping out as they lose their cards, until one player has captured all the cards.

Fish

A game for two or more players, but with preferably no more than nine in any group.

Four cards are dealt to each player, the remainder of the pack being placed face down in the centre of the table. From the player on the left of the dealer, and following in clockwise direction, each player in turn asks the one on his left for a card to pair off with one in his hand making, for example, two sevens, two Aces, etc.

As each pair is made it may be placed face down on the table. When a player does not receive the card for which he asks, he is told to 'fish', whereupon he must take the top card from those in the centre of the table and add it to his own hand.

If a player receives the card he asks for he is allowed to ask again until being told to 'fish', when the next player takes his turn.

When all the cards from the centre of the table have been taken the players continue asking the one to their left for a card until the whole pack is paired. The first player to get rid of all his cards is the winner.

Old Maid

Any number may play this favourite game. One Queen is removed from a pack of cards which is then dealt. The object now is to pair off the cards, pairs once formed being placed face down on the table.

In a clockwise direction from the left of the dealer, the first player holds out his hand of cards, fanned out and faced downwards, to the second player. The second player takes one card from the offered hand, adding it to his own. The second player then holds out his cards to the third player and so on. Any card taken which matches one in the hand to which it is added, forms a pair, e.g. two fives, two eights, etc. Eventually, all the cards will be paired except the one odd Queen. The player left holding this card is the 'Old Maid'.

The game may be restarted, and the player who is made 'Old Maid' the least number of times is the ultimate winner.

Donkey

Another suitable 'rest' game in the middle of an energetic party.

Each player has four cards, so thirteen players would be the ideal number to dispose of a complete pack. For each number less than thirteen a set of four cards is removed from the pack, e.g. if only ten players, then four aces, four twos and four threes may be extracted. When the cards are dealt, a signal is given and each player takes a card from his or her hand, passing it face downwards to the player on the left. The card received by each player is added to his or her hand.

The object is to obtain four cards of a kind, i.e. four nines, four fours, etc. As soon as such a set is collected, the player quietly places the cards face downwards on the table and sits with arms folded.

The remaining players immediately do the same despite the fact that they do not have a complete set of cards. The last player to notice that a set has been made, being the loser, takes the first letter of DONKEY (D). The game is repeated until one person has lost six times and is 'DONKEY'.

ANSWERS

Games in which the players must answer or reply

Nursery Rhyme Quiz:
(for the younger children)

The children are divided into two groups, each of which is asked a question concerning a nursery rhyme. For example:

'Who kissed the girls and made them cry?'
'In what did the old woman live who had so many children she didn't know what to do?'
'Who went to the cupboard and found it bare?'

The questions may be put openly to each group in turn, or alternatively, to individual team-members.

General Knowledge Quiz

By varying the degree of difficulty, this can be adapted to suit any age group. Organise two teams, questioning each in turn. Questions to be asked may be spontaneous, or pre-arranged, but it is advisable to have a reference book handy.

Scoring: For each correct answer, a point is gained for the team. A question unanswered, or incorrectly answered, may be repeated to the next member of the opposing team.

Alphabet Elimination

The players sit in a circle. A category is chosen, e.g. Christian Names. Each member in turn is then required to give a name commencing with 'A'. This could be 'Arthur, Anne, Alan, Amy', etc. Any person failing to supply an answer is eliminated. Any category may be chosen, e.g. Animals, Towns, Cities, Flowers, etc. and any letter of the alphabet. The choice, however, should not be altered in mid-circuit.

Complete the Proverb

This may be played individually, or by two teams. A player is given part of a proverb which he must then complete, for example:

It's no use crying over	– spilt milk.
People in glass houses	– shouldn't throw stones.
Better the day	– better the deed.
A rolling stone	– gathers no moss.
Look before	– you leap.
Pride comes	– before a fall.

He who hesitates	– is lost.
Set a thief	– to catch a thief.
It's a long road	– that has no turning.
A stitch in time	– saves nine.
It's no use closing the stable door	– when the horse has bolted.
A bird in the hand	– is worth two in the bush.
There's no smoke	– without fire.
An apple a day	– keeps the doctor away.
Time and tide	– wait for no man.

It is advisable to make a list of proverbs before the party. A scoring system similar to that for General Knowledge Quiz might be used.

Character Quiz

A game for two teams, each answering a question in turn, the questions being based on well known characters of fact or fiction, for example:

Who laid down his cloak before a Queen?
Sir Walter Raleigh
Who had tea with the Mad Hatter?
Alice
Who robbed the rich to aid the poor?
Robin Hood
Whose name is associated with November 5th?
Guy Fawkes
What crime did Guy Fawkes commit?
Treason
Who is associated with the Seven Dwarfs?
Snow White
Who was the distraught Lady who cried,
'Out, out damned spot'? *Lady Macbeth*

Who created Mickey Mouse?
  Walt Disney
Who offered his kingdom for a horse?
  Richard III
Who was banished to Elba?
  Napoleon Bonaparte
Who wrote a story whose hero was Huckleberry
  Finn? *Mark Twain*
Who discovered Newfoundland?
  John Cabot
Who sat on a tuffet and was frightened by a
  spider? *Little Miss Muffet*
Who was the first American in space?
  Col. Glenn
Who is the detective hero of Conan Doyle's
  stories? *Sherlock Holmes*
Name the Scotswoman who helped Bonny Prince
  Charlie in his escape. *Flora MacDonald*
Who was the elusive character the French sought
  here, there and everywhere?
  Scarlet Pimpernel
Who hurriedly left a ball at the stroke of mid-
  night and lost a slipper? *Cinderella*
Whom did President Kennedy succeed?
  President Eisenhower
Who was the creator of the Mona Lisa?
  Leonardo da Vinci

Prepare the questions before the party, using
characters suitable for the age group of the children, i.e. nursery rhyme and fairy story characters
for the young, and historical, fictional and present
day characters for older children.

QUIZ GAMES (7—11 YEARS)

1. Which of the following comes from Holland:
Tulips, Chalk or Beef?
Tulips

2. Is New York in North or South America?
North America

3. Does a group of cows form a flock, a herd
or a gaggle?
Herd

4. How many persons play a duet?
Two

5. Who is President of the United States?
President Kennedy

6. In which capital is the Eiffel Tower?
Paris

7. Was Charles Dickens an author, scientist or
musician? *Author*

8. What are the colours of the French Flag?
Blue, white, red

9. What two colours when mixed together produce orange?
Yellow and red

10. Who uses a lasso?
A cowboy

1. What is the currency of the U.S.A.?
The dollar

2. Is the tomato a fruit or a vegetable?
Fruit

3. What is the name of the garment worn by the
Ancient Romans?
Toga

4. Which people are Tomahawks?
   North American Indians
5. What are Saturn, Mars and Venus?
   Planets
6. Which is the odd one out: cows, horses, sheep, lions, pigs?
   Lions
7. Give another name for Satan.
   Devil
8. Who slept for 100 years to be awakened by a kiss? *Sleeping Beauty*
9. Which country is the home of the Koala Bear?
   Australia
10. Where is the Kremlin?
    Moscow

QUIZ GAMES (11—14 YEARS)

1. What ship was sunk on her maiden voyage by an iceberg?
   Titanic
2. Give another phrase for 'crossing the Equator'.
   'Crossing the line'
3. Where is the 'White House'?
   Washington, D.C.
4. How many tentacles has an octopus?
   Eight
5. What status is held by the Wife of the U.S. President? *First Lady*
6. Who is the head of the Roman Catholic Church? *The Pope*
7. Name the national game of America.
   Baseball

8. Where were the first Atom bombs dropped?
   Hiroshima, Nagasaki
9. What is the simplest form of life?
   Amoeba
10. What is pumice stone derived from?
    Lava

1. What is the number of the house in which the British Prime Minister lives?
   No. 10 Downing Street
2. How many Continents are there?
   Five
3. Name them.
   America, Asia, Australia, Africa and Europe
4. What is the name of the first Astronaut?
   Major Gagarin
5. What is his nationality?
   Russian
6. Name the fastest type of plane.
   Jet
7. Name the world's highest mountain.
   Everest
8. Where is it?
   Tibet
9. Is the whale a mammal or a fish?
   Mammal
10. In which American town are films made?
    Hollywood

BOARD GAMES

Board games have been in existence for more than four thousand years. We know this from excavations of ancient drawings on stone tablets, found alongside the remains of their wealthy owners.

The board game that simulates war seems to be the earliest, and historians have produced evidence of primitive peoples sketching out a 'playing surface' on sand and rock and using pebbles, flints, shells, plants, and seeds as 'men', moving them along lines or in squares and circles trying to 'capture' their opponents.

From these humble beginnings, chess originated. The exact date is uncertain but it is somewhere between 68o B.C. and the fifth century of our own era. Most writers on the subject agree that chess is to be traced to India, where the original chess-men represented chariots, horses, elephants and foot soldiers. Called the Indian Army Game, it was taken by merchants to Persia, where the modern game was developed. Rules and regulations were drafted and the pieces took on the shape we know today.

The majority of our popular board games have a long history which invariably goes back to ancient Egypt, Mesopotamia, Assyria, Cyprus, Crete, Greece and Asia generally. Dice are used with many of them: throwing dice is one of the oldest games in civilisation, invented, they say, by Palamedes in Greece about 1244 B.C.

Draughts

Draughts is an absorbing game, easier to master than Chess, but demanding some concentration, bluff, cunning and ability to be 'one step ahead!' Played by young and old, there are any number of variations using the same board and darughtsmen.

It is quite easy to make your own set. On a sheet of paper of about 14 inches square, rule off a series of 1½ inch squares—64 in all. With black paint, crayon or ink, fill in the bottom left-hand square and then every alternate one, working upwards in rows, so that you have a square board sub-divided into sixty-four equal white and black squares. When play begins, each player must have a black square on his left hand. Paste the paper on to strong board and give the surface a coating of transparent spirit varnish. For the draughtsmen you will need 12 white and 12 black pieces which

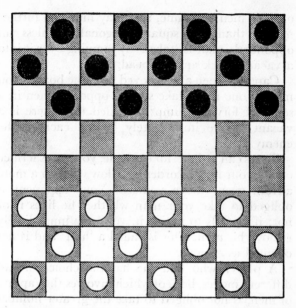

Draughts (Fig. 1)

can be made of thick cardboard or, with a little more trouble, of wood. (See fig. 1).

The game is for two players who sit opposite each other; one chooses the black 'men', the other the white, and these counters are always placed on the first 3 rows of the black squares nearest to the players.

The aim of the game is to 'capture' all your opponent's men or, alternatively, to force him into such a position that he cannot make a move.

Black begins by moving one man forward into another black square. Players may only move one of their men at a time, and may move no further *forward* than one square diagonally, unless an opponent's man is 'taken' by jumping over it into a vacant black square ahead.

Captured men are removed from the board. You may in one move take several opposing men in a series of forward jumps provided that there is a vacant square immediately behind each of the enemy.

Traps can be laid: for example, you may sacrifice one of your men in order to follow up with a more advantageous move yourself. Your opponent is obliged to take your man whether he likes it or not; if he fails to notice it, you may immediately remove his man. This is called a 'huff' and is not counted as a move.

A player who finds he has the choice of two different moves, both of which involves the capture of men, is not obliged to take the greater number and may elect to choose the smaller for reasons of his own. In this case, he cannot be 'huffed' for he could not, in any event, have made two moves at the same time.

As soon as a player's man reaches one of the four black squares on the far edge of the board, it becomes a 'King' and is 'crowned' by having another man of the same colour placed on top. Kings may move forward or backward, capturing opponents if there are vacant black squares behind or in front of them. Kings are vulnerable since they can also be taken by the opposing men.

There are no 'second thoughts' in draughts. You must forfeit the whole game if you touch a man and fail to move him, or if there is an opportunity of taking more than one of your opponent's men and you only take one; as soon as you have withdrawn your hand from the board you cannot go back to complete the 'move'.

There are a number of books which can be studied if you wish to fully master the tactics of this game.

Reverse

If the object of draughts is to capture all your opponent's men as quickly as possible, in Reverse, (as the title suggests) the object is exactly the opposite.

The first player to lose all his men is the winner, and this is by no means as simple and straightforward as it sounds.

Go Bang

A game for two players, who choose to be either white or black. The first player places a man in any square—black or white—and the other follows suit and places a man down in any unoccupied square.

The player who succeeds in getting five of his men in a straight line, either vertically, diagonally or horizontally, is the winner. One must try to position one's men to make it impossible for the opponent to use the free squares he needs. Should one hold the other so skilfully that by the time both have used up all their 12 men neither of them has achieved a straight line, then they may move their men about the board until one player does succeed.

Escape

One player has four black draughtsmen and the other player has a single white man. The four represent 'policemen', and the single piece an 'escaped convict'. The four policemen are placed along one side of the board on the black squares and the convict on any black square on the opposite side.

Policemen are moved first—always forwards—on any black square. The convict can be moved in any direction, but must not be lifted over any white square, for the game is only played on the blacks.

He must try to break through the police cordon. There is no 'taking' as in true draughts, but if the convict comes up against a policeman he must move off in another direction.

The policeman, as you will quickly discover, must be moved carefully, for should a gap be left the convict will be able to escape and win the game. But if the police can trap him so that he cannot move, then they win.

Chess

This game is almost as old as civilisation itself. To attempt to give a thorough grounding in this volume would be quite impossible: the subject is too vast. A student of this complex game must study some of the many books on the subject written by experts and masters.

Here we merely outline the object and purpose of chess, the pieces used in the game and their movements, value and power on the field of battle.

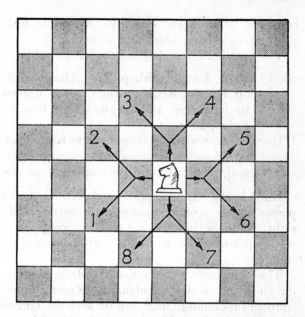

Chess – Possible moves of a knight (Fig. 2)

For chess is a miniature battle, waged between two armies each of 16 men with their own king and queen.

The field of war is the chessboard which, like a draughtboard, consists of 64 squares, alternately white and black, and arranged so that during actual play each player has a white square at his near right-hand corner.

Each side consists of one King, one Queen, two Castles (or Rooks), two Bishops, two Knights and eight Pawns. One side is white, the other black.

At the start of a game, each player stands his

complete team in the two rows nearest to him, using every square, black and white.

This is the order for battle from left to right:

Black: Rook, Knight, Bishop, King, Queen, Bishop, Knight, Rook, on the first row nearest to the player, and, on the second row, all eight pawns.

White: Rook, Knight, Bishop, Queen, King, Bishop, Knight, Rook, on the nearest row, and, on the second row, all eight pawns.

If the board has been positioned correctly (each player having a white square in the corner at his right) then the black King will be occupying a white square and the white King will be on a black square.

The following is an abbreviated code for identifying chessmen (which, incidentally, is used in most countries including Great Britain and the United States), and it is used in the majority of textbooks.

K – King; Q – Queen; R – Rook; KR – King's Rook;

QR – Queen's Rook; B – Bishop; KB – King's Bishop;

QB – Queen's Bishop; Kt – Knight; K Kt – King's Knight;

Q Kt – Queen's Knight; P – Pawn.

Pieces to the right of the King are called King's pieces (e.g. King's Rook) and pieces to the left of the Queen are called Queen's pieces (e.g. Queen's Bishop).

Other abbreviations to note include:

ch. – check; dis. ch. – discovered check; e.p. – *en*

passant; o–o–o: 'Castles' on the Queen's side; o–o: 'Castles' on the King's side; X indicates 'take'.

On the board, horizontal squares are called 'rows' or 'ranks', and vertical squares are 'files'. At the start of the game, each square takes the name of the piece which occupies it. For example, the square on which the King stands is called the King's Square or K 1. All other squares leading forward from K 1 are numbered 2 to 8. Therefore, the square immediately in front of K 1 is K 2, in front of that K 3, and so on along the file to the end square opposite which is K 8. The same applies to all the other pieces in their respective files (Q1, Q2 to Q8, etc.).

Thus each square has two names: one for the white men and one for the black. White's K 1 is also Black's K 8 whilst Black's K 1 is also White's K 8, and so on.

Abbreviations of this kind enable the various moves to be written down more easily. For example, we may now be able to decipher the following:

Kt to Q B 3

which means:

Knight to Queen's Bishop 3.

The whole object of Chess is to force your opponent's King into submission. Whilst the King is the only piece never actually 'taken', the game is over when the King cannot escape and the next move would have resulted in his capture. This is called 'checkmate'.

Now for the powers of each of the pieces:

The King: the game's most important piece, he moves in any direction to any one adjacent square and, if there is an undefended opponent on that square, it is taken.

The Rook (or Castle) can only be moved horizontally or vertically (i.e. along files or ranks) for any distance, taking any opponent which is in its path.

The Bishop: whereas Castle cannot move diagonally, Bishops must move diagonally and take opponents in their path. And they must also remain on squares of their own colour. They can move any distance, providing the path is clear.

The Queen can be moved diagonally, horizontally or vertically and is considered the most powerful piece.

The Knight moves in a somewhat complicated manner—one square to the side and then two forward, or vice versa. Thus with each move it changes the colour of its square. It is the only piece which can move *over* any piece of its own or opposing colour. (See fig. 2).

The Pawn moves forward in its own file only, one or two squares on its first move, one square thereafter. But the pawns can only 'take' on diagonals, and they may alter their normal straightforward course to do this.

Pawns can also take opponents *en passant;* that is if, when starting, a pawn moves two squares and passes an opposing pawn which could have been taken had it moved only one square, the opposing pawn has the option of taking it. If it does, this must form part of its next move.

Two versions of Apple Piercing —
a traditional Hallowe'en game

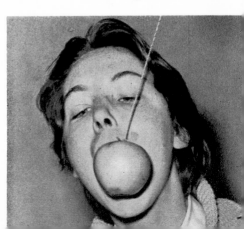

Two of the oldest board games—chess and draughts —
enjoyed out of doors

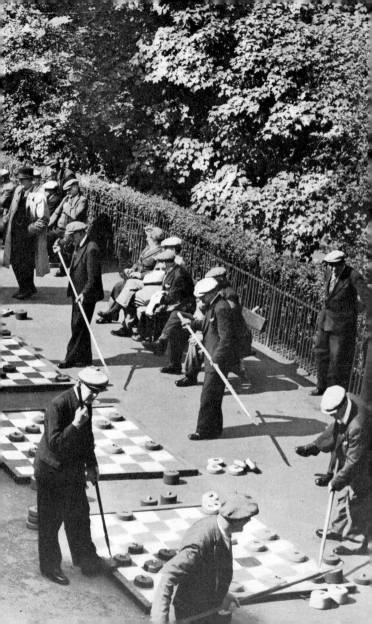

Friendly rivalry over the darts board in a typical English pub

Cribbage

In much the same way as draughtsmen are crowned when they reach the other side of the board, so pawns, if they reach the eight rank, are promoted to either a Queen, Knight, Bishop or Rook, whichever the player chooses. In practice, however, this is always a Queen or a Knight, for a Queen can perform all the moves of both Bishop or Rook.

But unlike draughts, one man is never lifted over an opponent in order to 'take' him. In chess, a capture is made merely by occupying the square on which the opponent is standing.

Finally here are some terms which are commonly used in chess:

Check: when a King is being attacked, 'check' is called. This is a warning that the King is theoretically vulnerable and must at once move out of 'check'.

Checkmate: the end of the game. The King, having been 'checked' cannot escape from check in any direction. This ends the game.

Stalemate: a drawn game when neither side wins, being unable to force checkmate, or because of 'perpetual check'. There are many other ways of reaching a stalemate, and these are listed in all the chess manuals.

Castling: Once during a game, the King, in conjunction with either Rook, is permitted to move two squares left or right with the Rook then hopping over the King to his far side. The King cannot 'Castle' if in check, or if this involves moving into check. Neither can he cross a square commanded by an opponent.

Tuppenny Ha'penny Football

Two pennies, one ha'penny, two combs and two pieces of wire are all that are required for this exciting table version of Association Football. A formica topped kitchen table makes an ideal playing surface.

Bend the wire into goalposts of any appropriate size and then make a clip at the bottom so that the 'posts' will slip on to each end of the table-top and remain reasonably firm. (See fig. 3).

Two players each take a penny (one should be bright and new, the other dark and older, or one penny can show 'heads' and the other 'tails'). Having decided who shall kick-off, the ha'penny (the ball) is placed in the centre of the table, the kicking penny close to it. The opponent must place his coin two inches away.

To set the ball in motion, a player hits his penny with a comb (or small ruler or stick) so that the penny, in turn, hits the ha'penny. Play continues in this way with the players taking turns. Should a player miss the ha'penny with his penny, he is not penalised—it is all part of the fun of the game.

These rules should be observed:

(a) if A's penny hits B's penny before touching the ball, B is awarded two shots in succession.

(b) If A's penny knocks B's penny right off the edge of the table (without having previously touched the ball), B has two 'free' shots from the place where his penny left the table.

(c) If A's penny knocks the ball off the table, it is a 'throw-in' for B who replaces the ball and takes one shot. To defend this, A can place his

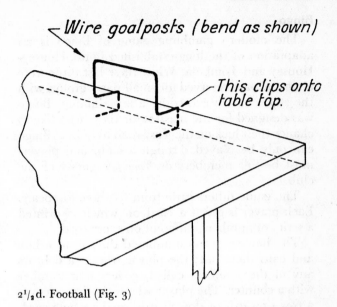

←Wire goalposts (bend as shown)

This clips onto table top.

$2^1/_2$ d. Football (Fig. 3)

penny anywhere on the table.

(d) If A's penny knocks the ball behind his own goal-line (a straight line running through the base of the goalposts to the edges of the table) it is a 'corner kick' to B. B places his penny in the corner with the ball immediately in front of it. A can place his penny wherever he likes.

B is then permitted two shots in succession.

Other rules can be framed to keep the game as near to the real thing as possible.

A goal is scored when one player succeeds in propelling the ball with his penny through the wire posts. With a little practice, angled shots and 'in-off' shots become possible.

Bingo

The modern gambling game of Bingo is an adaptation of the long-established Lotto, Housey-Housey and Tombola. While these last three were almost always reserved for small party groups with the stakes rarely exceeding a few shillings, Bingo was designed for the masses: for those who like to chance their luck on the 'easy road to riches.' Bingo can only be played through a club, and players must be full members or *bona fide* guests of the club.

The game differs little from its three forebears. Each player is given a card on which is printed a series of numbers, different on every card.

The banker draws numbered discs from a box and calls them out; the player whose card bears any of the numbers called, covers that number with a counter. The player who is the first to cover a row upwards or downwards, or the whole card, wins a stake of the pool.

Lotto, Housey-housey and Tombola invariably use cards with 15 numbers on them, ranging from 1 to 90. Bingo, the modern counterpart, has cards with 25 numbers on each (including one marked 'free play'), ranging from 1 to 75. The possible combinations in each case run into millions, but, generally speaking, the numbers produced average around 2,000.

Each player purchases a card and, under the British Betting and Gaming Act, the total intake constitutes the prize money which has to go back to the players. The excitement lies in winning the stakes.

The competitor who first covers his whole card is said to have a 'full house' and he wins a stake. But there are also prizes for those who first cover a line across the top and a line down the centre ('T for Tom'); a top line, middle line and bottom line (a 'sandwich'); any one line across ('one liner'); a line in a diagonal direction (a 'diagonal') and the top, bottom and side lines (a 'picture frame').

Over the years, the jargon of the callers has been part of the special fascination of Lotto and Housey-Housey. Bingo too has its own special language; the following are some of the most popular phrases:

KELLY'S EYE ....No.	1
LITTLE BOY BLUE	2
UP A TREE	3
ON THE FLOOR	4
JACKS ALIVE	5
BOX OF TRICKS	6
UP IN HEAVEN	7
AT THE GATE	8
DOCTOR'S ORDERS	9
COCK AND HEN	10
OH THOSE LEGS	11
ONE DOZ	12
UNLUCKY FOR SOME	13
ONE AND FOUR	14
ONE AND FIVE	15
SHE WAS SWEET	16
ONE AND SEVEN	17
ONE AND EIGHT	18
ONE AND NINE	19
ONE SCORE—BLIND	20
KEY OF THE DOOR	21

Snakes and Ladders

Up the ladders, down the snakes: that's the main point in this popular party game, which can be bought complete at any toy shop, although the more enterprising of you will design your own board, providing as many 'lucky breaks' (ladders) or as many 'big drops' (snakes) as you like.

Usually two take part although any number may. Each in turn throws the dice and move along the squares according to the number scored. If you land at the foot of a ladder you may climb immediately to the top and so forge ahead. But if you land in a square containing the tail of a snake you must drop back downward as far as the snake twists and turns. The first to reach the last square (home) wins.

Backgammon

This ancient British game (the name of which means, simply, 'back game') requires a special board, similar to that shown in the accompanying diagram. Made of wood, it consists of two equal compartments which open out at the centre on hinges. These two compartments are called 'tables' (one the 'outer' and the other, the 'inner') and are made up of twelve narrowly pointed patterns, alternately black and white, numbered 1 to 12, top

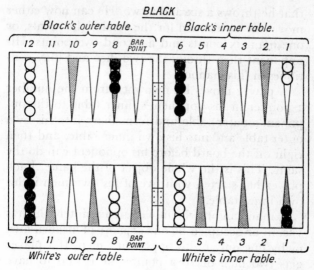

Backgammon (Fig. 4)

and bottom, with the 7th point commonly called the 'bar pointer'.

Fifteen white and fifteen black draughts pieces are arranged as in the diagram: White has two men on Black's number 1 pointer; five on his own number 6 pointer; three on his own number 8 pointer and five on Black's number 12 pointer.

Black has two men on White's number 1 pointer; five on his own number 6 pointer; three on his own number 8 pointer and five on White's number 12 pointer.

The first player throws two dice: let us suppose

that he throws a six and a two. He can now either move one of his men for the total eight points, or one man six points and a second two points. His opponent then throws the two dice and play continues in this manner.

A player moves his own men from the number 1 pointer in his opponent's inner table to the opponent's outer table and from there into his own outer table and into his own inner table, and then right off the board before his opponent can do the same. This is the whole object of the game. Each player has started with five of his own men in his own inner table.

A man can only be moved to a pointer which is vacant or occupied by one or more of his own men or by one only of his opponent's men. If a player gets two men on to a pointer he is said to have 'made' that pointer.

One man only on any pointer is called a 'blot', and if the opponent 'hits' it, he is said to have 'hit a blot'. He may then pick up the man and put it on the bar between the two hinged tables where it remains until it is played into the opponent's inner table during some future throw.

Whilst a player has a man on this separating bar, he cannot move any of his other men until he throws a number which tallies with a vacant pointer on his opponent's inner table.

Should a player throw the same number on each dice (for example, two fours or two sixes) this is called a 'doublet' and he scores double the total (i.e. for two fours he may move one or more men

16 points; two sixes enable him to move 24 points).

Having succeeded in getting all his men into his own table, he then 'bears them out' (starts to remove them from the board in order to finish the game). He is entitled, with every throw, either to move forward a man or men within his own table or remove men from the corresponding points. When a player throws a number with no man on it, he must play forward. However, if he throws a number which he cannot move, he bears off a man from the highest occupied point.

A victory is called a 'hit' if a player wins whilst his opponent has got all his men into his own home table and has also started to 'bear off'.

A 'gammon' is a victory where the winner has born all his men off before his opponent has begun to do this.

A victory is called 'backgammon' when the winner has born off all his men whilst his opponent still has a man (or men up on the separating bar or in the winner's home table). In this event, loser usually pays three or four times the agreed amount of a single stake.

Matches are the best of three: i.e. three 'hits', or a 'hit' and a 'gammon', or one 'backgammon'.

This somewhat complicated game is simpler if you follow the instructions carefully with a board and men set out in proper positions in front of you. (See fig. 4).

Familiarise yourself with the positioning of the men and their power to move before you challenge an opponent.

Bagatelle

This is a Billiards-like table game played with nine balls (one black, four white and four red) on a table 10 ft. long by 3 ft. wide into which have been sunk nine hollows or cups (See layout in fig. 5).

The holes are numbered (as is shown) and the object of the game is to 'hole' as many of the balls as possible, scoring a higher total of points than one's opponent.

There are many alternative games using bagatelle equipment, hence the various colourings of the balls, but we shall keep to the one involving the basic principles of the game.

Two players take part and each will need a cue (although sometimes a mace is used in a golf-swing action). The first player places the black ball on the spot indicated in the diagram (a) and then, on spot (b), places any other ball and propels it with his cue, as in Billiards aiming at the black ball. If it misses the black, it is removed from the table as are all succeeding balls until the black is played. If any ball rebounds back more than half-way down the table, it is also removed. Once the black is hit, the player may then place the balls anywhere behind spot (b).

Players must 'hole' as many balls as possible, each cup into which the ball lands counting for a different score. Black counts double.

Once the black has been holed (each player tries to get it into number 9 so that it counts as 18 points) all the remaining balls are hit into the highest possible holes. As in Billiards, they may go in off

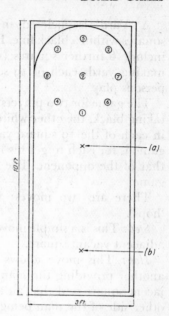

Bagatelle board (Fig. 5)

the surrounding table cushion or in off another ball.

When the first player has used up his balls, he notes his score and his opponent takes over. 'Game' is won by the player who is first to score 120 points.

Halma

The name stems from the Greek word meaning 'Leap' which describes the two principal moves of the game.

This game is played on a board which has 256 squares, and using 'men' similar to the Chess pawn. 4 persons may play, but the game is better with two players.

A 'Yard' is enclosed in each corner, i.e. 13 squares within a black line. Diagonally, two corners include 6 further squares (within a heavier line), making yards each of 19 squares used when two persons play.

The game for two players: each has 19 men, one taking black, the other white, and these are played in each of the 19 square yards. The object of the game is for each to get his men from his yard into that of the opponent. The first to do so wins the game.

There are two moves: (a) the 'step' (b) the 'hops'.

Step: This is a simple move in any direction to an adjacent vacant square.

Hop: This move allows a man to jump over another providing the man is standing on an adjacent square and that an adjacent square on the other side of the man being jumped is vacant and in the right direction. A hop may consist of one or more jumps, direct or zig-zag.

A player may jump over his own men and in fact places his men so that he can do this, and so that his men reach the opponent's yard as soon as possible. In assisting his own men, a player contrives at the same time to obstruct his opponent's progress. Men are not 'taken' in this game. To prevent your opponent gaining over your men, have breaks between them so that your opponent cannot advance in one continuous 'Hop.'

When 4 play, each has 13 men, their counters being black, white, purple and green. These are placed in the smaller yards. Each of the four may play for himself, or in two partnerships. If the latter, partners may sit opposite each other or side by side. By sitting opposite each other, each can better assist the other to yard his men. Whichever method is used, the object is for one partnership to yard their men before the others.

Go Bang

This game came into the British Isles from Japan, and there is no taking or moving involved. Though quite simple, it is fascinating and requires skill.

Two or four may play, though the game is most interesting for two players. A board of 361 squares (19 × 19) is used and each player has counters of a different colour.

Nothing is set on the board until the turn of the first player who places a counter on any square of his choice. The second player does the same and so the game continues. The object is for each player to place a row of five consecutive counters. The first to do so wins the game. The row may be diagonal, vertical or horizontal. (This game may also be played on a Draughts board, see p. 51).

DICE GAMES (FOR ADULTS)

Crap Shooting

A popular dice gambling game for two or more players. Two ordinary dice are used, and a coin is tossed to see who starts. The first player puts a number of chips into a central kitty and an equal amount is contributed by the others. He then rolls his two dice.

He wins all the stake money if with his first throw the sum of the spots on the two dice equals *seven* or *eleven* (this is called a 'natural').

He loses all the stake money if with his first throw the sum of the spots on the two dice equals *two*, *three* or *twelve*.

After this the man with the dice makes a fresh wager and throws again. If his first throw results in none of these totals, it follows that he will either score *four*, *five*, *six*, *eight*, *nine* or *ten*.

Each of these totals is called a 'point' and he must throw again to try to score another 'point'. For example, if with his first throw he scores six, he must then try to roll another six to win the stake money. He may need to throw a number of times to get his second six, but if a seven turns up in the meantime, he will lose all the stake money—and he must forfeit the dice. The 'turn' passes to the player on his left.

On the other hand, if a six (or whatever number he needs) does arrive before a seven, he wins the stakes and keeps the dice for another turn.

Poker Dice

Based on the card game, Poker, there are many variations of this game for two or more players.

With one popular method, you need a set of special poker dice (there are five, each marked Ace, King, Queen, Jack, ten and nine). Each player in turn rolls all five dice at once, trying to get a combination which ranks in the same order of merit as in the card game:

1. Five of a kind.

2. Four of a kind.
3. Full House (three of one denomination, two of another).
4. Sequence (five dice in a sequence; high sequence beats low).
5. Threes (three dice of the same combination; high beats low).
6. Two pairs.
7. One pair (high pair beats low pair).
8. Highest single dice—Ace high. (Ace with high backers beats Ace with low backers).

A player may have three throws. He can either leave all five as they turned up at first throw; throw them all twice again, or leave any number of them and roll the remainder. This is done in an effort to improve the combination.

The player with the highest combination wins the whole kitty, formed by each player matching the first player's stake, as in the crap game. The winner rolls first in the next round.

There are many variations of dice poker including one in which a player rolls and keeps the dice covered with his hands. He calls out the combinations to the others who must decide whether he is bluffing or telling the truth. In much the same way as in card poker (see appropriate section under Card Games) bets are laid, and other players may challenge him by paying to 'see' him.

Poker dice may also be played with five ordinary dice. Each player in turn rolls all five dice at once to get the best possible combination, the values of which (highest first) are:

1. Straight Flush: all five spots in sequence (e.g. 1, 2, 3, 4, 5; 2, 3, 4, 5, 6; 5, 4, 3, 2, 1 or 6, 5, 4, 3, 2).
2. Four of a kind (e. g. four spots of the same value).
3. Full House: three spots of one value, two of another (e. g. three ones and two fours).
4. Flush: all five spots of same value (e.g. five sixes).
5. Threes: three spots of same value (e.g. three fives).
6. Two pairs.
7. One pair.
8. Highest spot – six high (six with high backers beats six with low backers).

The player with the best combination wins the pool.

Aces

For any number of players from two to five (five are best). The five specially marked poker dice are used and each player, in turn, rolls all five dice at once. The aim is to roll five aces with the least number of throws, and win the kitty.

Whenever an ace turns up, it is left and the remaining dice rolled until all five are showing aces.

Boston

A number of chips are placed into the kitty and each player in turn rolls three ordinary dice together. The dice with the highest number showing is left, and the other two are rolled again. If after the first throw, all the dice show the same number of spots,

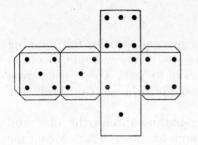

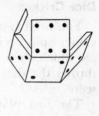

Make-a-dice (Fig. 6)

or two of them do, he may take any two and roll again.

After his second throw, he leaves the higher of the two and rolls the last dice again.

The total score of spots on the three dice after three throws is credited to him. Now, in turn, the others throw and the one with the highest total wins the kitty.

DICE GAMES (FOR JUNIORS)

Making Dice

Fig. 6 shows how you can make simple cardboard dice. Draw the shape on a sheet of card, making the squares about three-quarters of an inch wide and drawing in each square the dice-spots as shown.

Cut it out and bend into shape as shown and glue together.

Instead of drawing five dots in the top square, write the word 'OUT!' and you will have a special dice for the game 'Dice Cricket'.

Dice Cricket

You need two or more players for this amusing game. Split up into two teams and spin a coin to see which team goes in to 'bat'. The batting team throws the dice and the fielding team keeps the score.

The first player batting throws the dice and continues to do so until he throws 'Out'. Meantime he is credited with the number of 'runs' he scores. When the batsman throws 'Out!' the 'fielding' team should decide whether he has been bowled, caught, run-out, etc. When all the batsmen have thrown 'Out!', their opponents then go in to bat by throwing the dice.

Play proceeds as in real cricket.

This game can, of course, be adapted to baseball.

Soccer-in-Squares

A dice game for two or more players who should be divided into two teams. All you need is dice, a tiddly-wink counter (or small coin) and a special pitch.

The pitch is seen in fig. 7 and can be drawn to almost any size, preferably on cardboard.

Spin a coin to see which team will play UP the pitch and which team will play DOWN the pitch. The team losing the toss kicks off from the centre-spot.

To kick-off, place the 'ball' (counter or coin) in square 17 and throw the dice. If your team is playing UP, you must *subtract* the number of your throw from the number of the square on which the ball is resting. On the other hand, if your team is

2	5	GOAL 1	3	4
6	7	9	10	8
11	13	15	14	12
16	19	⑰	20	18
21	24	22	25	23
26	29	27	30	28
32	34	35 GOAL	33	31

Soccer-in-squares (Fig. 7)

playing DOWN, you must *add* the number of your throw to the number on which the ball is resting. For example, if the ball is on square 17 and a DOWN player throws a 3, he moves the ball to square 20.

Should a throw exceed number 35 (the goal) or be less than number 1 (the other goal), the opposing team place the ball in the square immediately in front of their own goal and take a goal kick from that spot by throwing the dice and continuing the game.

When a team has scored a goal (by landing the ball exactly into the goal square) then another kick-off follows.

A game should last for about 30 minutes—fifteen minutes each way. At half time the players change sides—the UP players become DOWN players, and vice-versa.

Centennial

Two players take turns to throw three dice at once with the aim of scoring from 1 to 12 and then 12 back to 1 again. To do this, they add together the spots on any two dice, or on all three, or they may only be able to make use of the spots showing on one of the dice. For example, in order to start a player must include a 1 in his throw. Let us suppose he threw two ones and a five. One of the 'ones' is counted, then by combining the two ones he gets two. The five is of no use to him. Suppose his opponent throws 1–2–4 with his dice. By combining the various spots he can count 1, 2, 3, 4, 5, 6 and 7.

Players start each new turn from the point where they ended last time. First to reach 1 to 12 and back to 1 again, wins.

Dice Pontoon

This is a suitable party game for any number of players. A dice is required and an equal number of counters per person. A kitty is formed by each player donating one counter.

In turn each player shakes and shoots the dice. Each attempts to score 21 in all and may shoot the dice as many times as he needs to achieve this total. Should his score exceed 21, he 'busts.' A player may 'stick' at a score below 21, for example at 18 or 19 when the risk of 'busting' is considerable.

At the end of each round, the player scoring 21, or nearest, wins the 'kitty'. If there is a tie, this can be played off.

Beetle

This is a simple game, but suitable for all ages, especially a mixed group. A dice and container are required and each player is given a 'Beetle' card or a sheet of paper and pencil.

Each in turn shake and shoot the dice. Drawing of the beetle cannot commence until a 6 is thrown, when the body may be drawn. Each subsequent 6 thrown, entitles the player to another throw; 5 permits the head to be drawn; 4 one antenna; 3 an eye; 2 a leg; 1 the tail. The winner is the first to draw a complete beetle.

Beat the Clock

Three or four players may take part in this game. A container and two dice are required. The object of the game is to progress from 1 to 12 in order.

Each in turn shake and throw the dice. Both dice may combine to score any number from 2 onwards.

Example: If 3 is required, this may appear on one of the dice, or the dice may show 1 and 2 which combine to make 3. In the same way, 2 may show on a single dice, or each dice show 1 and 1 equalling 2. The first player to reach 12 wins.

ADULT PARTY GAMES

INTRODUCERS

No doubt some of your guests will know one another, but some may be meeting for the first time. The object of the following few games is to mix your guests, enabling them to become acquainted with each other, and to start off your party with a swing.

Self-introductory Circle

The players form a circle in which the host joins. They then number off from the host in a clockwise direction. The host calls out two numbers, for example '2 meet 10, 6 meet 18', etc. As each pair is called, they step into the circle giving their names to each other and to the company. This continues until all guests have introduced themselves.

Nosey Parker

For this starter, two circles are formed—ladies on the inside, gentlemen on the outside. The ladies move clockwise, the men in the opposite direction. A few bars of music are played. When the music stops, players turn to face each other, and, having found his or her partner, rapid questions are fired and as quickly answered, each guest trying to learn as much about the other as time allows.

Circle of Inquisition

This introducer is very similar to Nosey Parker in procedure. The music is allowed to play and stop several times, to permit a number of separate introductions. Each time the leader selects a couple at random and asks them to relate what they know of each other. This continues until all the couples have had the opportunity to meet one another.

Autograph Hunter

Required: a card or piece of paper, and a pen or pencil for each guest.

Each player has to obtain the signature of all the other guests. He should be given a target number so that he or she knows when all the guests have been met.

Duplicates

Allow one slip of paper per person, with exactly the same wording on each pair, for example: 'Painting, Riviera, Apple' or any object that comes to mind.

Give one set to the boys, the duplicates to the girls, then invite guests to 'find your partner'.

Song Groups

Select some well known songs and, on separate pieces of paper, write down their titles, allowing one title to about every four guests.

Each guest is given a slip of paper containing a song title and is required to find others holding the same title. When groups have been formed, each in turn signs its appropriate song.

Opposites

Prepare slips of paper on each of which is written one of a pair of opposites, for example Night/Day, Sun/Rain, Hot/Cold, Wet/Dry, etc. Each gentleman is provided with one slip and directed to find the lady holding its opposite.

Jigsaw Partners

Before your party, prepare jigsaw pieces as follows: have half as many pieces of paper as the number of guests expected. Cut each piece of paper in two with a differently shaped cut each time.

One piece of each shape is given to a gentleman, the other to a lady. Each then looks for the matching piece.

Affinities

Compile a list of affinities, i.e. pairs of words which commonly go together, like 'in and out', 'knife and fork', 'this and that', 'here and there', etc. Write the first word on one piece of paper, the second word of the pair on a separate piece of paper.

Equip each of your guests with one half of a pair, a man with the first word, for instance, and a lady with the second. Each guest must then find his affinity.

Who am I?

Prepare a card for each guest on which is written the name of a famous character of fact or fiction, past or present.

On arrival, each guest has a card pinned to his back without seeing it, and he must question other guests in order to discover what name is on his card.

Untangle Your Partner

Distribute tangled lengths of string about the room and furniture, leaving the ends free.

Each guest takes an end and proceeds to disentangle his or her piece of string, the men taking opposite ends to the ladies. Partners will meet at some point along the line of string.

Who Fits the Slipper?

A shoe is taken from each girl. The shoes are then placed in a pile in the centre of the room. At a given signal, the boys each take a shoe and must then try to find its owner.

MUSICAL GAMES

Music required for these games may be 'live', (if someone plays the piano) or from gramophone records or tape recordings.

Musical Groups

All the players walk round the room in time to music. Whilst the music is playing the leader calls out the name of a musical group, for example: 'Octet, Duet, Septet', etc. As soon as the music stops, the players must try to form a group, or groups equivalent in number to the one called. Those left out of a group are eliminated.

Musical Box Forfeits

Players sit in a circle, around which a box is passed (a small sweet-tin is ideal). In the box are slips of paper, each containing a forfeit. When the music stops, whoever is holding the box at that time is required to open it, take out a slip of paper and perform the forfeit described. See page 140 for a list of ideas for forfeits.

Keep Your Seats

As many chairs as there are players are placed in two rows, back to back. The players walk in circle formation round the rows of chairs while the music plays. When the music stops, they continue in the same direction, each player returning to his original seat. The last one to sit down must from then on remain seated for the rest of the game. The last player left in circulation is, of course, the winner. Turning *back* to one's chair (having only just passed it) is not allowed.

Musical Relay

A game for two, three or four teams. A small

object such as a balloon or an orange is needed for each team.

The teams stand facing each other, forming a horseshoe shape if three teams, a complete square if four teams. The objects are placed in the centre of the area within the teams so that each team is at an equal distance from its object. In relay formation, each team member takes up the object in turn, returns to his team, and passes the object to the next player who then returns it to the centre. When the second player has returned to his team, the third player collects the object and so on. Any person found in possession of the object when the music stops loses a point for his team (a certain number of points having been allotted to each side previously).

Musical Follow My Leader

Players are seated and, as the music plays, the leader walks towards several people in turn. Each one approached by the leader must join in behind him. When the music stops everyone rushes to a chair, the last one to be seated paying a forfeit.

Musical Bonnets

Novelty hats for all but one player are required.

The players sit in a circle, all but one wearing the party hats. As the music plays, they pass their hats around the circle, and when it stops each player immediately places a hat on his head. The player left without a hat is out of the game. As each player is eliminated, one hat must also be removed.

Musical Prize Parcel

Make a large parcel with numerous separate wrappings tied up with string, the first wrapper containing a small prize. Here and there a forfeit may be inserted.

The players sit in a circle and, as the music plays, the parcel is passed round. When the music stops, the person holding the parcel must try to unwrap it, passing it on again when the music restarts. Anyone turning up a forfeit must perform it as described. The prize goes to the person who succeeds in removing its wrapper.

NOVELTY DANCES

Dances introduced between games are always popular. For the following, no particular type of dance is necessary.

Elimination Dance

The dancing is stopped at varying intervals, the object being to eliminate couples from the floor. The last couple on the floor is the winner. Each time the music stops the host announces what will disqualify a couple from continuing in the dance. The following are just a few examples:

1. Any man wearing shoes without laces.
2. Those who ate porridge at breakfast.
3. Men without watches.
4. Girls wearing more than three articles of jewellery.
5. Men who have more than 12 loose coins in their pockets.

6. Men wearing brown shoes.
7. Girls without grips or hairpins in their hair.
8. Any man carrying matches.
9. Girls with blue eyes.
10. Men wearing shirts with unattached collars.
11. Girls wearing green.
12. Any couple having danced the last three dances together.

Colour Elimination

The room is divided into four or more imaginary sections, each of which is given a colour. Music is played, and when it stops, a colour is called and all those in that particular area must leave the floor.

Spot Dance

In this dance when the music stops, all stand still and the couple nearest to a pre-determined area, or object, are the winners who qualify for a prize. Alternatively, a second neutral person may be given instructions such as: 'Take four paces, turn left, take two steps backwards, right about turn and touch the nearest couple on your right.' The couple touched is the one eligible for the prize.

Statue Dance

As the music stops, all couples must remain in whatever position they are at that precise moment. Anyone detected 'moving a muscle' is eliminated. This continues until only one couple remains. Alternatively, while the music plays, certain positions or guises may be announced, to be adopted when the music stops. Here are some examples:

1. Stand on the left foot with the right arm raised.
2. Adopt the pose of ballet dancers.
3. Men kneel on the right knee, girls sit on their left knee.
4. Pose of Spanish dancers.
5. Pose of guitarists.
6. Man carrying girl across river.
7. Bell-ringers.
8. Artist and model.
9. Man bows, lady curtseys.
10. Highland Fling.

Excuse Me Dance

This may be a Men's, Ladies', or General dance. In the former, men who are not dancing, but wish to dance with someone already on the floor, may do so by approaching the partner and saying 'Excuse me'. A 'Ladies' Excuse Me' allows a girl to displace any other girl on the floor. In a 'General Excuse Me', both sexes are allowed to break in. The displaced partners then find others and continue to dance, the object not being to eliminate couples, but to mix people up.

Snowball Dance

One couple commences the dance and, when the music stops, the partners separate and each selects another partner. The dance continues in this manner until all 'sitters out' are included.

Paul Jones

Partners take the floor for normal dancing, but when the music changes to a march the girls must form an inner circle, the boys an outer circle. The girls move round clockwise, the boys anti-clockwise. When the music stops, each dancer takes the nearest partner for the next dance. All types of dances may be incorporated in the Paul Jones, which is a good 'mixer', encourages the timid, and provides an excellent start to a party.

ACTIVE GAMES

Contests

The following are games which feature individual ability, each player competing against the others.

Putt the Balloon

One inflated balloon, spherical or elongated, pencil and paper, and a tape measure are required.

Mark out a line, from behind which each player in turn must throw the balloon as far as he can; the distance is then measured from the line to the spot where the balloon first touches the floor. A judge jots down each player's name and putting distance. The player who succeeds in throwing the balloon furthest is, of course, the winner.

This game may also be played with other light objects, such as a drinking straw, handkerchief or playing card.

Pennies in the Well

Required: a waterproof sheet or square, a good supply of pennies, a 2 lb. preserve jar submerged and standing upright in a pail of water.

Each contestant drops pennies into the water,

aiming them into the jar. A set number of attempts are allowed, the one with the most pennies in the jar being the winner. This may not sound difficult, but it will be found that the pennies tend to 'drift' in the water.

Keep the Plate Spinning

Required: one tin or enamel plate.

The players sit in a fairly open circle, each being allowed a number. The game commences with one player standing in the centre of the circle. He sets the plate spinning and calls out a number. The player with that number must catch the plate before it falls flat, set the plate in motion again and call out another number, and so on. Any 'number' called who does not reach the plate before it falls, or who knocks it over, is eliminated. Any spinner calling a number already eliminated is also disqualified.

Pile On

A game of manipulative skill. One bottle and a quantity of matchsticks are required.

The object is to pile the matches across the top of the bottle opening without causing any to be dislodged. Each player in turn adds a match to the pile. Anyone causing a match or matches to fall is eliminated, the player left in at the end being the winner.

Blow the Ball

A ping-pong ball and tape measure are required. This game is similar to 'Putt the Balloon'. Form a starting line. Allowing one blow per person, each player has to blow the ping-pong ball as far as he can. When the ball comes to rest its distance from the starting line is measured, and the winner is the one who achieves the greatest distance.

Stool Quoits

One upturned four-legged stool and four quoits are required.

From a distance of approximately 10 ft. each player throws the four quoits in turn, aiming to 'ring' each leg of the stool.

Scoring: allow one point for each leg ringed and a bonus of five for ringing all four legs. The highest scorer over a pre-determined number of attempts is the winner.

Six Hole Bounce

A small cardboard box, in the base of which six adequate holes have been made, and one ping-pong ball are required.

The upturned carton is placed on the floor. Each player in turn then aims the ball to bounce off the floor into a hole in the box. If successful, a point is scored. Allow each player an equal number of attempts, the highest scorer being the winner.

Burst the Balloon

Each player is supplied with an uninflated balloon. At a given signal, each player commences to blow up his or her balloon until it bursts. The first to burst a balloon is the winner of the game. To make the contest a little more difficult it may be ruled that only one hand may be used.

Target Line

Each player requires a set number of disc-shaped objects, such as halfpennies, pennies or draughts.

From a distance of approximately 10 ft., each player in turn slides a coin toward the target line, which is a chalked line or a crack between floor-boards or table boards. After everyone has made an attempt, the one whose coin is on or nearest the line wins all the coins. The game continues until one person possesses all the coins in use.

Magic Square

A piece of cardboard 12 in. × 12 in. divided into nine numbered squares, is required, and objects such as draughts, coins or crown corks.

The board is placed flat on the floor approximately 10 ft away from the players. Each player in turn has a set number of throws, aiming the objects on to the board, the highest points scorer being the winner. Any object falling clearly into a square scores the number in that specific square. Should an object touch or overlap any line, no score is recorded.

Newspaper Jumble

One newspaper is required for each contestant, each of the same size and with the same number of pages.

Thoroughly jumble up the pages of each news-paper. The contestants are seated round a table, or in a circle allowing limited space for any movement. Newspapers are distributed at a given signal, whereupon each player is required to arrange his paper into proper order. The first to do so correctly is the winner.

Putting

A golf club (putter), an umbrella or walking stick, a golf, ping-pong or tennis ball and a basin or small pail are required.

The receptacle is placed on its side. From a distance of approximately 10 ft. each player in turn attempts to get the ball into it in as few strokes as possible. Allow a set number of 'holes' (say nine), the winner being the player who has taken the least number of strokes.

Relay Races

The following are games in which two or more teams compete. However, almost all relay races may be run or adapted as individual contests, the object in either case being *speed*.

Chopsticks

Required: one bowl, or saucer, and one pair of knitting needles per team. To each bowl, allot as many grains of rice as players per team.

Players form teams and when the starting signal is given the first member of each team tries to remove one grain of rice from the bowl, using only the needles (as chopsticks). Having done this, he then passes the bowl of rice and needles to the second player. The whole procedure is repeated by all the team, the first to finish being the winner.

Paper Clip Chain

Teams of equal numbers are arranged. Each team leader has two paper clips, and the remaining players one paper clip each.

On the signal to start the leader joins together the two paper clips, passing them to the second player, who adds his clip. Each succeeding player adds his clip to the chain which, when completed, is taken to the leader by the 'anchor man' who then goes back to his place. The leader now starts to reduce the chain by removing one paper clip. This reduction continues along the team to the last player, who will receive two clips to be separated. The first team to complete the procedure wins.

Chin Chin

Required: one round object per team, for example a ball, orange, or apple.

Arrange mixed teams, ideally, boys alternating with girls. The ball is held in place under the chin and the aim of the game is to pass it along the team members and back in this manner.

Rules: 1. Use of hands is not allowed except to replace the ball should it fall to the ground.
2. Should the ball fall to the ground the passer must replace it under his or her chin.

Variety Motion

A game for two teams which sit facing each other a reasonable distance apart. One player at a time, first from one team and then the other, moves down the space between the two teams, each player proceeding in a different manner, e.g. walking on all fours, walking crabwise, skipping, hopping, etc. Any player repeating the movement of another, or failing to perform when called upon, is eliminated. When all players have had their turn the team with the fewest number of players left is the loser.

Paper-round

Required: one piece of thin paper 4 in. to 6 in. square per team, and one drinking straw per person.

The teams form circles. Each leader starts the game by placing the straw in his mouth and inhaling to hold the paper to the straw. Then, without using hands, each player, inhaling through his drinking straw, receives the paper from the previous player and turns to pass it to the next. As one player breathes in, the other breathes out to help the paper on its way. Should the paper fall, it may be picked up by the hands, but with skilful performers it is more fun to rule that the paper may only be retrieved with the straw.

Stepping Stones

Required: numerous books, magazines, pieces of cardboard or newspapers per team. Average newspapers should be folded to a quarter of their size.

Each player is required to go over a set course, stepping on the books or papers only, advancing one at a time.

Nose the Ball

Required: one table and one ping-pong ball per team. Equal teams are formed, and the game is to propel the ball with the nose over a certain course, such as along one edge of a table and back. In the latter case, opposite sides of a table can be allotted to two teams.

Rules: should the ball leave the table it must be replaced at the point from where it fell.

As each player completes the course he returns to his place, handing the ball to the next team member. The first team to finish is the winner.

Nosebox Race

Required: one matchbox cover per team.

Equal mixed teams are formed. The leader fixes the matchbox cover on his nose. When the signal to start is given, the matchbox cover is passed along the team from nose to nose. Depending on the number of players in the teams, the game may finish either at the last team member, or when the matchbox cover has passed back to the leader. Use of hands is not allowed, except to replace the matchbox cover if it falls from the nose.

Dead and Alive

Required: two matchboxes and an equal number of used and unused matches per team.

Teams of equal number stand or sit in line. The leader has a matchbox containing unused matches, the team player at the end of the line having the used matches in a second box. At the signal to start, the leader passes down the live matches one at a time. Simultaneously, the dead matches are passed up the line in the opposite direction. The first team to get the matches completely and correctly transferred is the winner.

Tied in Knots

Required: one long piece of thick string or rope per team.

After a starting signal has been given, the team leader ties a knot in the length of string, then passing it to the second player who does the same and so on down the team. The game may finish at the last man, or continue with each player being required to unfasten a knot, ending with the length of string restored to its original form.

Mock Football Pass

Required: one balloon or small ball per team.

Teams are seated side by side in lines. The object is to pass the ball along the team on the upper side of the feet. Should the ball fall to the floor, it may be retrieved only by the feet. Use of hands is not allowed.

Thread the Beads

Required: one length of thread, and an equal number of beads in a container for each team.

A knot or bead is tied at the end of each piece of thread. Teams of equal numbers are formed. A starting signal is given and the leader begins by threading a bead, then passing beads and thread to the next player, who does likewise. The first team to thread all the beads, wins.

Poise

Required: one book per team.

Each player must travel a set course, balancing the book on his or her head, without touching the book with the hands. Should the book fall to the floor, it may be replaced on the head, but meanwhile the player may not move forward.

Spoon the Potato

Required: one spoon and one potato per team.

A starting line is marked across a set course. Teams of equal numbers form behind the line, and a spoon and potato are placed in front of each team. On the starting signal, each player in turn tries to manoeuvre the potato into the spoon, without the aid of fingers or feet, and then carries it over the course and back. The first team to finish wins.

Glove Inversion

Required: one chair and one pair of gloves per team.

Teams of equal numbers form behind a starting line. A chair and gloves are placed parallel with, but a set distance from, each team. Each player has to run to the chair, turn the gloves inside out (or outside in, as the case may be) and return to his place. He is followed by the other members of the team. The winner is the first team to finish.

Goad the Orange

Required: one orange, one short cane or stick, and one chair per team.

Place the oranges and canes on the starting line in front of each team and the chairs at a set parallel distance. Each player has to steer the orange along the course by prodding or tapping with the stick, passing it through the chair legs, and back to the starting line.

Bottle Balance Transfer

Required: one chair and three or four bottles, with necks narrower than their bases, per team.

Place a chair an equal distance from each team and the bottles standing upside down on the floor at the left of the chairs. Equally numbered teams form behind the starting line. Each player in turn runs to the chair, sits on it and proceeds to transfer the bottles to the opposite side of the chair. The bottles must be balanced, standing base uppermost. Having completed this task he returns to his place and the next player takes a turn.

Spoon Feeding

Required: one spoon per person and one ping-pong ball per team.

The teams form into equal lines or circles. The object is to pass the ball into the spoon of the next player all along the line.

Rules: 1. Spoons must be held in the mouth at all times.
2. Use of hands is not allowed.
3. If the ball drops it must be picked up by the passer using only the spoon, which must still be retained in the mouth.

Miscellaneous Races

The following games are for teams and pairs which are not in relay formation. Speed, however, remains the objective and decides the winner.

Top Dog

A game for two teams of equal numbers.

Required: any object to serve as a bone, for example a small book, ball, or an actual dried bone.

The teams sit or stand facing each other not less than 7 ft. apart, and number off from the right. The bone is placed on the floor, in the centre between the teams, and a referee takes up a position between the teams but outside the area of play. The referee then calls out a number, for example '7', whereupon the opposing players of that number must try to get the 'bone' to their own team. When one of them has picked up the 'bone' he must quickly return with it to his place. The opposing player, however, must try to tag him before he reaches his place.

Rules: 1. A tag can only be made whilst the 'bone' is being held by an opponent.
2. It is not permissible to *throw* the 'bone' to one's team.

Scoring: a point is scored each time a player successfully delivers the 'bone' to his place without being tagged. Alternatively, a player successfully tagging his opponent gains a point.

The game continues in this manner, the bone being replaced each time. The winner is the first team to reach a pre-arranged total of points.

Blow Football

A game for two teams, played on a table.

Required: four small books, one drinking straw per player and one ping-pong ball.

The books serve as goalposts and are placed approximately 6 in. apart, two at each opposite edge of the table. The 6 in. gap between the books represents the goal or target area.

All the players stand around the table, each team keeping to its own half of the table and so forming a semi-circle around its own goal.

Each team tries to score points by blowing the ball into the opposing goal by use of the straw alone.

Rules: 1. At the start of the game, or restart after the ball leaves the table, the referee must place the ball in the centre of the table.
2. Pushing and any blowing that is not through the straw, is not allowed, the penalty being a free blow at goal to the opposing team.

Ties and Sashes

A game for mixed pairs.

Required: one tie, and one length of ribbon or material as a sash for each pair.

After the starting signal each boy puts the sash round the girl's waist, fastening it with a neat bow at the back. *At the same time* the girl puts the tie round the boy's neck, knotting the tie in the proper manner. The first couple to complete this double task wins.

'I must have'

This game may be played with two or more teams, each having a leader. A neutral player stands at the same distance from all the teams and calls out, one at a time, for various objects, for example, 'I must have a ballpoint pen, signet ring, collar and tie, etc'. Any one of the team members may provide the object, but only the leader can take the object to the 'caller', and the first to do so scores a point. The game continues until a team scores a set number of points or, alternatively, the winner is the highest scoring team after a set time.

Sir Walter Raleigh

This is another game for mixed pairs.

Required: two pieces of old cloth, or folded newspaper, approximately 12 in. square, for each couple.

The boy in 'Sir Walter Raleigh manner' places the papers or cloth in front of the girl. She then steps on them, one at a time. Each couple covers a there-and-back course, the one doing so in the shortest time being the winner.

Crab Walk

A game for partners, each couple requiring a ping-pong ball or similar small round object.

Each couple covers a course with the ball held between their foreheads. Hands must be kept behind the back. The first couple to cover the course without dropping the ball is the winner.

Miscellaneous Games

Most of the following games are played simply for fun, and require no special competitive skill.

The Swatter

This is a game with a hoax. For maximum effect it should be allowed to proceed authentically for a while, before altering its nature.

Required: one thick rug or blanket and one swatter, which may be a folded magazine or newspaper.

Two players lie face downwards on the floor under the blanket, with their heads completely covered. The remaining players surround them, standing in a circle. The swatter is then passed round the circle, one player swatting one of the two blanketed figures and quickly passing the implement to someone else, or throwing it down to the floor. After being swatted, the victim emerges from the blankets to try to guess which player was his attacker. If he guesses correctly the two change places and the game begins again. If the guess is incorrect, the game continues as before.

The game continues for a time until, by contrived arrangement, a selected 'victim' becomes a centre player. At this point the game alters. Most of the swatting is now done by the second player *under* the blanket. To make it quite realistic, the second player should also be swatted from time to time. If after some time the victim does not guess the true identity of his swatter, be merciful and give some obvious hints.

Shake It Off

As with the previous game, this also is of the 'Red Herring' type.

Required: a small coin such as a sixpence.

The leader wets the coin and presses it firmly to his forehead. Then he shakes his head to remove the coin. Surprisingly, the coin at first adheres firmly to the skin, but eventually falls off.

After this demonstration, he invites other guests to try this act, the last of whom will be the victim. With this unfortunate player, the leader wets the coin and presses it to the victim's forehead, but removes it immediately. The victim will then go on shaking his head, possibly for some time, before realising what has happened.

Blind Man's Buff

This is a well-known game usually played at children's parties, but it can also be fun amongst adults. One player is blindfolded, spun around three times and then has to catch any player within his reach and try to guess his identity. The remaining players dodge about to avoid the groping blind man—the game being played in total darkness! Furniture adds to the fun, so long as it is of a stable and upholstered type.

Quick as a Wink

This is a game of alertness, also calling for guile on the part of the 'winker'. The girls are seated in a circle which includes one empty chair. Behind each chair stands a boy. To obtain a partner the boy behind the empty chair must wink at a girl who then quickly goes over to his chair. Each boy, however, may prevent the girl leaving him by lightly taking hold of her shoulders, but he only does this when his partner is the one at whom the wink is directed.

Each player must therefore be alert to detect the 'wink' and the 'winker' cunning. He may for instance direct his gaze to the left, then suddenly wink at a girl on his right. Following each successful partner-change, the one deserted becomes the 'winker'.

The game continues thus and, if desired, after a time you can change over so that the girls stand behind the chairs to try out *their* 'winking-ability'.

Initiation Ceremony

Required: two plates, one of which contains dry custard powder, cornflour or plain flour.

In this game there is a snare into which an unsuspecting victim is drawn. He (or she) is led to believe that the power to charm those of the opposite sex will be bestowed upon him. To achieve this power, however, he must first take part in an initiation ceremony which involves his being blindfolded and then kissing three times a plate with mystic powers.

The victim is permitted to see the empty plate, then he is blindfolded. The ceremony should be conducted with some imaginative 'hocus-pocus'. As the victim is about to kiss the plate for the third time, plates should be switched, so that the one presented for kissing is the one containing the flour.

Obstacle Course

A game in which there is a hoax.

Required: small objects for use as obstacles, for example, a small upturned pail, a pile of three or four books, a pair of shoes, a cardboard carton, a small mat.

Place the objects at intervals in a straight line on the floor. Volunteers are called for, one or two of whom will later be victims, though they are unaware of this. In turn, each player is instructed to cover the course twice, stepping over each article, but for the second circuit he is required to be blindfolded. When he is blindfolded the obstacles are quietly removed so that he strides over obstacles which are no longer there.

The hoax may be taken further by asking for another volunteer. He will assume that when he is blindfolded the obstacles will be removed but you can surprise him by leaving a few obstacles in place! To make this more effective, make a few significant noises as one or two articles are removed, so giving an impression to the victim that the course is being cleared.

Apple Piercing

This game seems to be traditional with Hallowe'en parties, but can prove equally amusing on any party occasion.

Required: one small tub or large pail containing water; some small apples which are set bobbing in the water; one fork per player; one chair.

Each player in turn kneels on the chair and clenches the fork handle between the teeth. He or she then leans over the tub, and aims to pierce an apple. If successful, the apple itself can constitute the prize.

Another version of this game is to attempt to secure an apple between the teeth by ducking the head into the pail or tub. Alternatively, apples can be suspended on string in a manner that enables them to swing and move freely. Keeping his hands behind his back, each player then attempts to eat an apple.

Complete the Donkey

This is one of the many forms of a favourite game.

Required: the outline of a donkey (minus tail), chalked on a board, or drawn on a large piece of paper or cardboard, and hung or pinned on a wall; one length of fairly thick string, with a drawing pin passed through one end, which serves as the donkey's tail.

Each player in turn stands by the wall opposite the outline. He is blindfolded, handed the tail at the drawing pin end and then turned around three times. He is then required to walk to the donkey and pin the tail correctly in place.

Invariably the tail is fixed to the wrong place, which provides a good deal of fun for the onlookers. Of course, any animal outline can be used for this game, and the part to be attached may be tusks, trunk, horns, whiskers, ears, etc.

Sardines

This is a fairly well known game, popular particularly with a mixed group of teenagers. Some power of detection is required of the players, but in the main, this is a game purely for amusement.

Initially, one member only hides. He or she may be told where to hide, preferably in such a place as a large cupboard, or small closet, or in any place where a number of persons can hide together, but becoming 'packed like sardines' by doing so. When the first player has hidden himself the second player is sent in search of him and instructed, on discovering the hideout, to hide with him. The remaining players are likewise instructed and sent off one by one at intervals. As more players squeeze into the hiding place, an added difficulty will be to suppress giggling in order not to give the game away to those still seeking.

QUIETER GAMES

In this section are games which do not require physical exertion, and these rest games can be sandwiched between those of a more strenuous type.

Miming Games

In these games, one or more players have to guess a word, a phrase or a situation, other players portraying the answer by using dramatic action, but not speech.

Dumb Crambo

A game of American origin for two teams. The challenging team selects a verb for the other team to guess and mime. Having selected the word, the challenging team gives one clue, which is a word which rhymes with the chosen one.

Example: the verb selected by the challengers is '*tip*'. The challenging captain then states: 'We want a word rhyming with 'sip.' The challenged team then list all the verbs rhyming with 'sip', for example, 'dip, rip, nip, whip, *tip*' and proceed to act them in mime. The challenging team loudly hiss and boo at all the incorrect guesses and clap and cheer when the correct guess is made. The teams then switch, the challengers becoming the performers.

Give the Title

Once again the players divide into two teams, one to act, the other to watch and guess. The acting team selects a title of a film, play, book or song, then acts it in mime. When the title has been guessed, the teams reverse rôles. The 'guessing' team may first establish the category into which the title falls, i.e. theatre, cinema, television, etc.

Guess the Situation

Each player, or pair of players, is given a situation to portray by action or pose, while the remaining players try to guess what the situation is. For example, a pair may be given one of the following: (1) A dentist and his patient; (2) A waiter and a difficult customer; (3) A tailor fitting a suit; (4) A customer purchasing a washing machine from a demonstrator; (5) An enthusiastic wife shopping with a reluctant husband; (6) An irate shoe fitter's assistant trying to please a customer who wishes to try on every possible pair of shoes in stock; (7) A ballerina and partner; (8) A timid suitor requesting of an austere father his daughter's hand in marriage; (9) A man laying lino and receiving well-meaning but by no means helpful suggestions from his partner; (10) A wildly cheering, gesticulating spectator alongside one who bears the brunt of this enthusiasm.

Some individual situations might be: (1) Boarding a bus with many parcels; (2) Obtaining stamps from a machine which is out of order; (3) A boy imitating a girl spotting a spider on her dress; (4) An adult portraying a very young child in a fashion parade; (5) A drunk trying to find his key and unlock a door; (6) A cook in a panic; (7) A new father changing a nappy; (8) A door-to-door salesman plying his wares; (9) Paper-hanging with great difficulty; (10) A very inexperienced farmhand milking a cow.

What Am I To Do?

In this game, one individual is the 'guesser' and he also mimes. This player leaves the room whilst the others decide amongst themselves what situation or action he is to perform on his return. The player must then try to solve the problem, not by asking questions, which are not allowed, but by miming various actions until he hits on the one required of him. The only clues other players may give him are those that hint how close he is to the right answer, for example, by calling out: 'You are cold, warm, warmer, hot, or very hot.'

Mime Race

This is a popular parlour game. The players divide into two teams, each of which elects its own captain. The leader has a prepared list of items to be mimed. These may be single words, phrases, titles, names of characters of fact or fiction, etc.

At a given signal, each team captain comes forward and receives from the leader a folded slip of paper on which is written the item to be performed. Each captain receives exactly the same phrase or word. The captains then return to their respective teams, read the wording on the slip of paper and proceed to mime it, the remainder of the team trying to guess what is being mimed. This constitutes a round. A correct guess concludes a round.

Each team then elects a new captain and another round begins, the new captains going to the leader at a given signal and receiving another item to be mimed. Thus, each player has an opportunity to mime.

Rules: hard and fast rules are not imposed, but some principal points have become generally accepted. The mimer may not speak—as in other mime games—but the team members may talk amongst themselves and to the captain. Although the captain cannot answer directly, he is allowed to nod or shake his head in response to questions. Also, he may make any gesture or action he chooses, provided this does not actually indicate a letter sign, i.e. writing in mid-air the specific word or word letter.

Scoring: the first team to guess correctly the item being mimed scores a point. At the end of the game, the team with the highest score is the winner. A time limit of five minutes may be set for each round. If neither team has made a correct guess at the end of five minutes, no score is made and the next round is begun. This game is best played in a fairly large room so that the two teams can be placed reasonably far apart.

Memory and Observation Games

In the following games, the powers of observation and/or memorising ability are brought into play.

Find the Treasure

Prepare lists beforehand of a number of articles to be found in one room. The articles listed may be complete objects, or something which is incorporated in another object. Each item should be detectable without anyone needing to move or touch anything in order to see it. For example, the list might include a handkerchief, which could be lying in a chair or apparently dropped on the floor, a flower woven into a cushion covering, or a part of a wallpaper design. Each player is provided with a list, which he completes by jotting down the location of each article. A specific time is set and the player correctly locating the most items is the winner. The players should not touch anything in the room, so that no article listed is moved.

Spot the Changes

Place ten small objects on a tray or table. Allow the players to observe these for twenty seconds and then cover the objects or remove them from the room. When the articles are again revealed, some of them should be placed in a different position (say upside-down, or half turned) or in a new place entirely. Each player is then required to describe the changes that have occurred. This can be done either verbally or in writing, the winner being the one who gives the most correct answers.

Up Jenkins (Tip It)

This is a game for two teams of equal numbers who sit at a long table, opposite each other. One team has a coin which it must keep concealed, and the opposing team has to find it.

The team with the coin passes it from hand to hand under the table. When so desired, the leader of the opposing team calls out 'Up Jenkins!' upon which the hands of the team passing the coin must all be raised simultaneously above the table, fists clenched.

At the command 'Down Jenkins!' the clenched fists are quickly lowered and the palms of the hands placed flat on the table. At this point, the opposing team must locate the coin. After consulting together the following orders may be issued, either by the leader alone or by each team member in turn.

If an outright guess is made the leader points to the hand of his choice and calls 'Tip it'. If this guess is wrong then the team with the coin wins a point, keeps the coin and starts the game again.

Another method is to eliminate the empty hands, leaving the hand holding the coin until last. As the leader, or another member of the opposing team, points to a hand, 'Take that hand away' is called. Should the coin be revealed by such a call, then the coin-holding team wins a point. When several hands have successfully been removed, an outright guess may be made if desired by calling 'Tip it'.

If a guess is not correct, the coin side wins a point, but if correct, the opposing team scores, claims the coin and begins the game again.

Scoring – One point per win and the team with the highest score after a set number of games is the winner.

Who Has the Ring?

Required: a long piece of string joined into a loop on to which a ring has been threaded. All the players form a circle, except one, who stands in the centre. Each member of the circle joins hands with his neighbours over the loop of string, the ring being clasped in the hand of one of the players. The ring is now passed from hand to hand along the string.

The player in the centre has to find out who is in possession of the ring by calling out a particular player's name or touching his or her hands. When correctly guessed, spotter and spotted change places. All the hands moving simultaneously make it harder to spot the ring, but to make guessing even more difficult the direction of passing the ring may be changed at will.

Observation (Kim's Game)

Place on a tray, or table, twenty or more objects. These are displayed to the players for one minute and then covered. Each player must then list from memory the objects he has seen, the one with the largest correct list is the winner. If desired, this game may be played as a team game, each team submitting one list to which all its members contribute. The amount of detail can be more elaborate if you decide to increase the difficulty of the game.

Who Is Leader?

This is a game of observation and detection. One player leaves the room; the remainder form a circle and elect a leader. The leader begins a movement such as swinging one arm, which all the others follow. Once the action is under way, the player outside is called into the room. At frequent intervals, the leader changes the movements, the other players copying whatever he does. Examples of movements are clapping the hands, tapping one shoulder, shaking an imaginary dice cup, etc. The odd player's task is to detect the leader. When this has been successfully done the two change places and the game begins again with the first leader leaving the room.

Who Is Missing?

This is a useful rest game as only two players are active at a time. One player leaves the room and a second player hides. The remaining guests sit or move around the room as they desire, the more natural their actions, the better. The first player is recalled and is then given fifteen seconds in which to name the missing person. If there are a large number of guests, more time may be allowed.

Name the Face

Previous preparation is required for this game. From newspapers or magazines, cut out faces of men and women (about ten in all) who are not immediately recognisable as famous personalities. Attach each picture to a separate piece of stiff paper or cardboard and number them. On separate slips of paper write out their names.

The faces are placed upwards on a table with the wrong name below each one. The players look at the pictures for three minutes and they then are removed. Each player now has to identify the pictures by their correct names, listing them in the order they are numbered. The player with the most correct list wins.

Snowball Actions

The players form a circle and the game commences with one player performing an action. This may be anything he wishes, for example patting his head, pulling his ear, stamping a foot, shaking an imaginary duster, etc. The next player copies the action of the first and then adds a different action of his own. The third player performs the actions of the two previous players, then his own. The game continues in this manner, each player performing the previous player's actions in their correct order and then adding his own. Should there be any fault, the player responsible may have a point scored against him, or be told to pay a forfeit. (See page 140 for list of suggested forfeits).

What Did She Wear?

One of the girls enters the room wearing distinctive clothes and carrying as many accessory articles as possible, for example, wearing a skirt, jumper, cardigan, short coat, mackintosh, shoes, hat, beads, brooch, bracelet; and carrying a handbag, vanity case, umbrella, scarf and gloves, etc. She remains in the room a few minutes, walking around and talking to guests, then leaves. Each competitor then compiles a detailed list of the articles worn. Allow ten minutes before scoring, awarding one point for each correct item and deducting two for any incorrectly named.

Pencil and Paper Games

For all the following games, paper, and pens or pencils are required. The host is also advised to have a dictionary handy to settle any arguments!

Consequences

This game is a popular favourite providing amusing results. Pencil and paper are required for each of the players who sit in a circle. The leader of the game calls out an instruction and the reply is written down by each player, who then folds over the paper from the top, covering the word or words just written. The paper is then passed on to the next player on the left, and so on, so every successive answer is written by each player on a different piece of paper. Instructions given could be as follows: 1. Write down an adjective. 2. Give a girl's name. 3. Another adjective. 4. A boy's name. 5. How did they meet? 6. Where did they meet? 7. What did she wear? 8. What did he wear? 9. What did she do? 10. What did he do? 11. What did she say? 12. What did he say? 13. What was the consequence? 14. What did the world say?

When the round is completed, each paper is read as a story, either by the leader, or by each player in turn.

Jumbled Proverbs

Some previous preparation is required for this game. Make a numbered list of proverbs. These are then written out in a jumbled or re-arranged form, either on a large scale for all to see or numerous smaller lists, allowing one list per player. Each player is then required to write out the proverbs correctly, allowing one minute per proverb, i.e. a period of ten minutes for a list of ten proverbs. The first all correct list, or the one with the most correct in that time is the winner. The following are examples.

| A rolling stone gathers no moss. | – Gather rolling a moss no stone. |
| Look before you leap. | – You before look leap. |

Barking dogs seldom bite.	– Bite barking seldom dogs.
He who hesitates is lost.	– Is who lost hesitates he.
It's no use crying over spilt milk.	– Spilt use over no milk crying it's.
People in glass houses shouldn't throw stones.	– In shouldn't houses stones people glass throw.
Pride comes before a fall.	– Comes fall a before pride.
Dog in a manger.	– A manger dog in.
You can't have your cake and eat it.	– Have and your can't eat it cake you.
Two are company, three a crowd.	– Are crowd a company two three.

Mixed Questions and Answers

This is a non-competitive game, played merely for fun. Each player is provided with two slips of paper and a pen or pencil. They write on one slip of paper any questions, and the corresponding answer on the other slip. All the papers are collected into two containers, the questions in one, the answers in the second. The containers are shaken and each player in turn draws out one question and one answer which he reads out aloud. The answer will seldom be at all related to the question, and the combination is often very amusing.

Step-words

This is an old game and still very popular. Players may participate singly or in teams. Each contestant is given a list of approximately five pairs of words. The idea of the game now is to change one word of each pair, until it forms the second word of the pair. One pair of words at a time is tackled and each word-change progresses in steps. The word being changed must be altered by only one letter at a time, and each alteration must form a new dictionary word. For instance, changing PEA to POD may be done as follows: – PEA-pet, pet-pot, pot-POD. Three steps have been necessary to change the word, and with each step a new word has been formed by altering only one letter, other letters retaining their set order.

The object of the game is, of course, to make the change with as few steps as possible. Using again the above example, by a more roundabout method the change might take five steps, i.e. PEA-pet-pat-pad-POD. The player who changes the most words in the fewest steps, within a limited amount of time, is the winner.

When preparing the step-words, it is best to use words of three and four letters—and each word must have the same number of letters as its pair. The following are samples, though not given necessarily in the fewest possible steps.

    GLASS-class-clans-plans-plane-PLATE
    HILL-hall-hale-DALE
    BLACK-slack-stack-stock-stork-store-stone-stole-stale-shale-whale-while-WHITE
    HARD-hart-haft-raft-rift-sift-SOFT
    EAST-past-pest-WEST
    LEAD-load-goad-GOLD
    FALL-fill-file-rile-RISE
    SHOE-shot-soot-BOOT

HAIR-lair-laid-land-band-BALD
STICK-stock-stork-store-STONE
LOSE-lone-line-fine-FIND
HIDE-hive-live-line-link-pink-pick-peck-
peak-leak-leek-SEEK
AIR-sir-sit-set-SEA
HATE-have-rave-rove-LOVE
FAIR-fail-fall-ball-bale-dale-dare-DARK
WET-wit-win-tin-ton-toy-try-DRY
COOL-coil-coin-corn-worn-worm-WARM

Drawing Blind

This game is played with the lights out—in total
darkness if possible. Each player requires paper and
pencil, and preferably should be seated round a
table, or with something firm on which to rest his
paper.

The players are asked to draw a simple object
such as a profile, head and shoulders of a man,
a tree, or frontage of a house. When all appear to
have finished drawing, the leader creates a diver-
sion by groping for a dropped pencil, or starting
small talk. As an afterthought, he then asks for an
addition to the drawing, such as spectacles, a hat,
or cigarette to the portrait, an owl in the tree,
a path to the house, or a figure by the house door.

The lights are then put on and all drawings
shown. The result is often as surprising to the individual artist as it is to the rest.

The Other Word(s) (Anagrams)

This game may be played individually, or players
can form small groups.

Each of the players or groups are given identical lists of words from which other words can be formed by rearranging and using all the letters. (Time, Mite, Emit, for example, are multiple anagrams of Item).

A limited time is allowed in which the players are required to write down anagrams of the given words. The first to supply a complete and correct list, or the one with the most correct in the given time, is the winner.

Examples: bale-able
diet-edit-tide
tinsel-listen-inlets-silent
post-stop-tops-pots
lemons-melons-solemn
verse-sever
live-evil-veil-vile
eats-east-sate-teas-seat
pram-ramp
miles-smile-limes-slime
rose-sore-eros
trap-part-rapt
pins-spin-snip-nips
pines-snipe-spine
cheap-peach
reap-pare-pear
over-rove
palm-lamp
balm-lamb
thorn-north
laps-alps-pals-slap
tips-pits-spit

pans-snap-naps-span
meat-team-mate-tame
capes-paces-space
simple-impels
untied-united
soup-opus
slow-owls
dimple-limped
lapse-pales
slope-poles-lopes
acre-care-race
rattle-latter

How Many Words (Dictionary)

This is a word-forming game. One reasonably long word having eight or more letters is selected. From the same word each player then forms as many other smaller words as possible. In forming a word, no letter may be used twice unless it occurs twice in the original word. For instance, from the word 'concentration'—concert, rate, nation, ration, rat, tin, trace, etc. can be formed. 'Concentrate', however, cannot be formed as the letter 'e' is required twice, but appears only once in the original. The formation of proper nouns is not allowed, and it is perhaps wise to stipulate a minimum of three- or four-lettered words. A limited time should be given, and the player with the longest correct list at the end of this time is the winner.

Guess From the Drawing

This is a game to be played by two teams, and requires one member of each team to draw something, the remaining team members being told to guess what it is. The items may be well-known phrases or proverbs, people, places, and/or events, titles of books, plays, films, songs etc. These should be selected in advance and each item written out on two separate slips of paper. Two temporary artists, one from each team, are handed the first item and they try to draw it for their team. They are not allowed to speak or mime, or to write down letters, words or figures. The other team members, however, may speak amongst themselves and to their artists, who are allowed to nod or shake their head to any guess or suggestion. The first team to guess the item correctly is awarded one point. Each team then elects a new artist, and the game continues as before. After a set number of items the team with the most points is proclaimed the winner.

Jumbled Words

This game may be played by groups, teams or individual players. In preparation, words in a certain category or categories should be listed. Sufficient copies are then made on slips of paper, but on these each word is jumbled.

When the game is played, a time limit is set in which each player, team or group, tries to write out each word in its proper formation. The first to complete the list correctly within that time, or the one with the most correct solutions is the winner.

FRUIT	FLOWERS	ANIMALS
Spegra	Liddffoa	Paloder
Grapes	*Daffodil*	*Leopard*
Ngeora	Yccnmeal	Erde
Orange	*Cyclamen*	*Deer*
Npepapiel	Esaferi	Gun
Pineapple	*Freesia*	*Gnu*
Arpe	Wawlflelor	Loin
Pear	*Wallflower*	*Lion*
Ananab	Oevitl	Taprenh
Banana	*Violet*	*Panther*
Lump	Etrsa	Raeh
Plum	*Aster*	*Hare*
Molne	Mropisre	Nxoe
Lemon	*Primrose*	*Oxen*
Neniagetr	Ladndnoie	Kydeno
Tangerine	*Dandelion*	*Donkey*
Rorogebeys	Noncatair	Toast
Gooseberry	*Carnation*	*Stoat*
Stade	Ylil	Tntike
Dates	*Lily*	*Kitten*

Send a Telegram

The leader dictates fifteen letters of the alphabet which may either be chosen at random, or may in themselves comprise one or more words. Each player then tries to compose a telegram of fifteen words. Each of the words he uses must commence with one of the dictated letters, and must be used in the order in which they were given. In judging, preference should be given to the one that shows the most originality, or raises the biggest laugh.

Oral Games

The following include competitive and non-competitive games, guessing games and games of repetition. In each, however, speech is the main activity involved.

Mixed Stories

This game requires somewhat tedious preparation, but pays dividends in laughter. In advance of the party, two stories are selected and written out in digest form. Short, well-known stories such as 'Goldilocks and the Three Bears' and 'Cinderella' are best. Each sentence of the two stories is written out on a separate slip of paper and put in a container. Before the game begins the slips are thoroughly mixed in the container. Each player then draws out one slip which he reads aloud when it is his turn. The result is a nonsensical, though amusing combination of the two stories.

Twenty Questions

In this well known game, one player selects in his own mind an object, preferably of a specific nature and likely to be familiar to the other players. Having decided on an object, he may, if he wishes, offer the information that his object is of an 'animal', 'vegetable' or 'mineral' origin, or a combination of these. The remaining players are then allowed to ask twenty questions in an effort to identify the object selected. The one being questioned need only answer 'Yes', 'No' or 'I don't know'. If a correct guess is made, the guesser is then entitled to select the next object, and the game recommences. If twenty questions are asked without the object being guessed, the same player reveals the correct answer and goes on to select another object, continuing until defeated.

Going into the City

This is an amusing repetitive game. The players seat themselves in a circle. The leader states that they are all going to the city, each taking an article for a special purpose. He then says: 'I am going to the city and will take my scooter'. The second player repeats that he is going to the city and will take another article, for example a horse, vegetables, umbrella, etc.

The third player then repeats, 'I am going to the city', etc. and introduces the article he will take. This continues around the circle until all have added their article.

The second round begins with the leader announcing what he intends to do in the city with his chosen article. For instance—'When in the city I will have my scooter serviced.' The second player then repeats the phrase, naming the article he selected in the previous round, as for example: 'When in the city I will have my horse serviced', 'When in the city I will have my vegetables serviced', and so on. As before, this continues round the circle.

The third round, however, is begun by the second player who may say, 'When in the city I will enter my horse into the Gymkhana'. The third player substitutes his article for 'horse' as follows—'When in the city I will enter my vegetables in the Gymkhana', etc. The game continues thus until each player has started a round, describing what they will do in the city with the article they take.

I Went Touring

This game is also repetitive but involves forfeits and mistakes. The players sit in a circle and the leader begins by saying 'I went touring and took my—', mentioning anything he likes, such as a camera, suit-case, bikini, etc.

The second player repeats exactly what the 'leader' has said but adds to it an article of his own selection. For example, 'I went touring and took my camera and my toothbrush', his own article being the toothbrush. Each player then in turn repeats all that has previously been quoted and adds his own article at the end.

Should any player make a mistake, he may be asked to pay a forfeit or have a point scored against him.

The introduction of one or two difficult items adds to the fun, for example, 'A book in which to note places of interest visited', or 'An extra one of everything in case of loss, accident or damage'.

Spelling Bee

Prior to the game, the words for spelling should be selected, easy ones to start with becoming progressively more difficult. The players form two teams and face each other in line, sitting or standing. A neutral leader controls the game and calls out the words for spelling. Each player in turn attempts to spell a word, the leader zigzagging from one team to the other, i. e. the first player of one team, then the first player of the second team, followed by the second player of the first team and so on.

If a player spells a word incorrectly, the same word is offered to the next player in the opposing team. If again incorrectly spelled the word is put to the next player in the first team, and so on until correctly spelled.

When a player spells a word correctly a point is awarded to his team, and the next player of the opposing team is given a new word. After one or more complete rounds the highest scoring team is the winner.

Spelling Bee Variation

This game is much the same as the previous one except that it is not a team game. Instead, players form one single line and spell words in turn. On mis-spelling a word, a player is eliminated and the same word is given to the next player. The game continues until one player remains, and he is the winner.

Spell Backwards

This game is not a spelling bee in the true sense, but requires an ability to call out the letters of a word in reverse order. The words selected for spelling should therefore be fairly simple ones.

The players are seated in a circle and each in

turn attempts to spell backwards a word called out by the leader. Any player making an error has a point scored against him or her. After a set number of complete rounds the player with the lowest points total is the winner.

Dictated Situations

This is a non-competitive game with amusing results. Three guests act as Dictators and the remaining players sit in a circle. One Dictator goes to each player in the circle and whispers the name of a person, who may be either fictitious or factual, for example, 'Tom'. Similarly, the second Dictator informs each player where the person can be found, for example, 'in a fireworks factory' or 'in a haunted house'. The third Dictator adds to each an occupation, for example 'making hot-cross buns' or 'planning to escape'.

Different information is given to all the players so that every player has a different name, place and activity. Each player then in turn states his own name and what he has been told.

Using some of the above examples the following might be announced: 'I am Mary Brown; I am with Tom Thumb in the firework factory, making hot-cross buns', or 'I am John Smith; I am with Brigitte Bardot in a haunted house, planning an escape.'

Baker's Dozen

In this game, players call out words. A circle is formed by all players except one who stands in the centre. The player in the centre selects a three-lettered word. He then points to a circle player, calls out the word, spells it, counts to twelve and then calls out 'Baker's Dozen'.

During this time, the player in the circle must call out three words, each beginning with the letters comprising the three-lettered word announced by the centre player. Also, the three words must be in correct letter-order. For example, the centre player may select the word 'map'. He points to A and says 'map, M-A-P, 1-2-3-4-5-6-7-8-9-10-11-12, Baker's Dozen'. Any dictionary word can be used. When counting, the centre player should pronounce the numbers distinctly. If a circle player fails to give three words before 'Baker's Dozen' is called, he or she changes places with the player in the centre.

Whisper

All players are seated in a circle. One player whispers a short sentence to the player on his left. The second player whispers what he hears to the third player, the third player to the fourth and so on round the circle. The last player is asked to say what he heard whispered to him and the first player is asked to call out his original whispered sentence.

The result may surprise you. Usually, the sentence changes as it is passed round the circle and in the end there is little resemblance to the original version. The famous example is 'Send reinforcements, I am going to advance', which becomes distorted to 'Send three and fourpence, I'm going to a dance.'

Murder

This is a guessing game, particularly popular with teenagers. The essential element is surprise, so the game should not be announced. Two players only should be aware that the game has been planned, they being the 'murderer' and the 'victim'. The victim, however, should not know who is to be 'murderer', nor the time and place that the murder will occur.

At some stage during the evening, (the murderer should be told when), the lights are extinguished. The murderer will be close to the victim and at his touch, the victim will scream. No doubt some confusion will follow, during which the murderer moves away from the victim. The lights are put on and everyone is asked then to remain exactly where they are. At this stage, one or two guests are selected to be detectives. They proceed to question everyone. All must answer truthfully except the murderer, who may tell as many lies as he can think up.

Skeleton Words or Ghost

This is an intriguing game in which words are suggested but not completed. The players sit in a circle and the game begins with one person thinking of a word of two or three letters. The first letter is announced and the second player must think of a word of not less than four letters which begins with the same letter. Having thought of a word, he then calls out the second letter of the word. The third player must now think of a word beginning with the same two letters. The game continues in this way, each player thinking up a word beginning with the letters already called (but a complete word must not be formed after he has added a letter).

The following is an example: the first player thinks of 'his' and calls 'H' (the first letter). The second player selects 'hard' and calls 'A' (the second letter). The third player thinks of 'hang' and calls 'N' (the third letter). The fourth player now must think of a word commencing HAN. He probably thinks of 'HANdsome' and would call 'D' (fourth letter). However, this would compose a complete word, i.e. HAND. The penalty is the loss of a life, each player having three lives. When all three lives are lost, the player must leave the game.

If a player is suspected of adding a letter without having an actual word in mind, he may be challenged. A player who loses the challenge loses a life.

To add amusement to the game those who are fully alive (i.e. those with no lives lost) are not permitted to speak to those partly alive (i.e. those with one or two lives left). If they do so, they themselves lose a life. Consequently, those with lives lost do their utmost to get the others to talk to them.

Granny Had a Cake

In this game, players think up appropriate verbs and call them out in alphabetical order.

The players sit in a circle and the leader says 'Granny had a cake.' He then goes on to give a verb beginning with 'A', as in the following example: 'I ate it'. The second player then repeats the statement substituting 'ate' with a verb commencing with 'B'. For instance, 'Granny had a cake. I bought it'. Each player in turn repeats the statement, but inserts a verb beginning with the next letter in the alphabet—such as 'I cooked it', I dropped it', 'I earned it', 'I flattened it', etc.

What Am I Doing and Where?

This is an oral guessing game for any number of players. One person selects a place and activity. They need not be related, and the more absurd, the more amusing the game will be. All the other players in turn then put forward questions to determine where the player is and what he is doing. For instance, he may choose to be trying on shoes in the middle of the High Street, or knitting socks during a balloon flight. Questions are answered only by 'Yes' or 'No' or 'I don't know'. The first player to make a correct guess then changes places with the one being questioned.

I Love my Love

This game is a word game requiring each player to name adjectives in alphabetical order. The players sit in a circle and the game commences with the first player saying 'I love my love with an A, because she or he is...' and here insert any adjectives beginning with 'A'. The second player then says 'I love my love with a B, because he or she is...' using an adjective commencing with 'B'. The game continues in this manner, each player naming an adjective which begins with the next letter of the alphabet. For instance, 'A' – adorable, 'B' – beautiful, 'C' – charming, 'D' – dainty, 'E' – exciting, etc. Should a player fail to produce an adjective he is eliminated and the next player continues.

The Last Becomes First

This is a word game. The players are seated in a circle. A category is selected, for example, animals, flowers, cities, etc. The leader begins the game, calling out any word in the selected category. If the choice of category was 'animals', the leader may call 'dog'. The second player also calls out a word in the category, but it must begin with the last letter of the leader's word. Thus he may call 'giraffe'. The third player then calls a word in the same category beginning with the final letter of the previous word; this may be 'elk'. The fourth player may then call 'kitten'—and so on.

A player repeating a word or failing to call a word is eliminated from the game.

Fizz-Buzz

All the players are seated in a circle and call out numbers. The leader commences with 'one', the player on his left 'two', the third player 'three', and so on. The numbers five and seven, however, may not be called. Instead, FIZZ is substituted for five and BUZZ for seven. This also applies to any number which contains any multiple of five or seven, or any number comprising these digits.

Example:

1	16	31
2	BUZZ	32
3	18	33
4	19	34
FIZZ	FIZZ	FIZZBUZZ
6	BUZZ	36
BUZZ	22	BUZZ
8	23	38
9	24	39
FIZZ	FIZZ	FIZZ
11	26	41
12	BUZZ	BUZZ
13	BUZZ	43
BUZZ	29	44
FIZZ	FIZZ	FIZZ

This game may be separated and played alone as FIZZ, which substitutes the number five. Alternatively, BUZZ only can be played, in which the number substituted is seven.

I Went Shopping

In this game, the players in turn call out nouns in alphabetical order. A circle is formed and the leader says 'I went shopping and bought...'—inserting at the end of the statement a noun beginning with 'A'. This may be 'aspirins', 'apples', 'artichokes' etc.

The second player substitutes a noun beginning with 'B'—'beetroot', the third 'C'—'cheese', etc. A player failing to name a noun, or incorrectly doing so, is eliminated and the next player continues the game.

Charades

This game is popular with all. A charade is built on a single word of two or more syllables which, when separated, form other words in sound, for example; abominable, a-bomb-in-a-bull; campaign, camp-pain or pane; servant, serve-aunt; abundance, a-bun-dance, etc.

The players divide into two teams. One team goes out of the room, selects a suitable word and plans scenes which bring in the syllables in order and finally the whole word. They then return to the room and briefly act each scene, the word sections being brought into the dialogue. The other team tries to guess the word, then the teams change rôles. If they fail to guess correctly, then the acting team selects and acts another word.

RIGMAROLE GAMES

In these games, words and actions are repeated over and over again.

Toast to Colonel Bogey

This game is played with the players seated round a table, each with a glass containing a drink. The leader commences the game as follows: Picking up the glass between thumb and first finger of the right hand, he pronounces the words, 'Here's to the health of Colonel Bogey'. He then drinks and replaces the glass on the table. He wipes the right side of an imaginary, or real moustache with his right forefinger, then the left side with the left forefinger. With the right forefinger, he taps the table to the right of the glass, then the left side with the left forefinger. Next he taps the underside of the table with the right forefinger, then with the left forefinger. Finally he stamps first his right foot, then his left foot on the floor, rises from his chair a few inches, and sits down again.

Each player in turn now duplicates exactly the first player's words and motions. When all have done so, the original player begins the second round. This is as the first except that everything is done twice. The glass is lifted between the thumb and two fingers and the words, 'Here's to the health of Colonel Bogey, Colonel Bogey' are said.

Two distinct drinks are taken from the glass and it is twice replaced on the table. The right side of the moustache is wiped twice with two fingers of the right hand, the left side twice with two fingers of the left hand. The table is tapped twice to the right of the glass with two fingers of the right hand. The table is tapped underneath twice with two fingers of the right hand, twice with two fingers of the left hand. The right foot is stamped twice on the floor, then the left foot twice on the floor. Rise twice from the chair and sit. As before, each player repeats this in turn. A third round is performed in the same way, everything being done in threes.

Uncle Joshua's Death

The players are seated in a circle and the leader starts the game by saying to the person on his left—'My Uncle Joshua died last night.' The player replies, 'That's too bad, how did he die?' The leader answers, 'with one eye shut' and shuts one eye which remains closed until the game is over.

The second player now turns to the third and says 'My Uncle Joshua died last night,' repeating exactly the same formula. This is continued round the circle, until each player has one eye shut. The leader then commences the second round, but when the second player says 'That's too bad, how did he die?' the leader replies 'With one eye shut, and his mouth awry.' He screws his mouth to one side. This is repeated round the circle. In the third round the reply to the question is 'With one eye shut, his mouth awry, and one foot held high,' whereupon a foot is raised and held in the air. In the fourth and last round, the reply is 'With one eye shut, his mouth awry, one foot held high and waving goodbye.' Each player has an eye closed, his mouth twisted to one side, a foot in the air and waves his hand.

Tom Thumb Fell Sick

This game is much the same as the last, but the words and actions differ.

The players sit in a circle and the leader begins the game with the player on his left, saying: 'Tom Thumb fell sick.' The second player asks, 'How did he get sick?' and the leader replies 'Doing this.' These words are accompanied by an action: in the first round this is patting the left knee with the right hand.

Second round – Patting right knee with left hand.
Third round – Tapping right heel on floor.
Fourth round – Tapping left heel on floor.
Fifth round – Nodding head back and forth.

Each movement is continued throughout the game so that in the last round five movements are being simultaneously performed by each player.

SUGGESTIONS FOR FORFEITS

1. Make a speech pretending to be a politician standing for re-election.
2. Recite a nursery rhyme as if you were a nervous child.
3. Say the alphabet backwards.
4. Sing a duet in soprano and bass parts.
5. Describe how to shave (for a woman).
6. Imitate a mannequin (for a man).
7. Have a conversation with an imaginary, deaf character.
8. Tell a funny story.
9. Describe how to make a macaroni pudding (for a man).
10. Describe how you would change a tyre (for a woman).
11. Imitate a temperamental artist.
12. Imitate a B.B.C. announcer giving a weather forecast.
13. Perform a Cossack dance.
14. Pretend to be a salesman selling perfume and give a persuasive sales talk, but through your gestures show how insincere your words are.
15. Pirouette round the room.
16. Imitate a dog with a bone.
17. Repeat 'Is this a myth Miss Smith?' rapidly.
18. Give a lecture on yesterday's news.

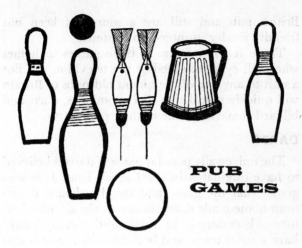

PUB GAMES

Britain takes pride in her 90,000 pubs and inns, with their folklore and atmosphere. The pub goes back to the Roman occupation, when the tribunes and their legions brought pitchers of wine by the boat-load and set up wine and ale-houses for their thirsty soldiers who drank, sang and played their games ('Tali' and 'Tessera' with dice of bone, and many board games). Ever since, the British pub has not only been a place to go and buy a drink, it has also been a recreation centre.

Darts was born in an English inn, whilst dominoes is a delightful pastime played in the friendly atmosphere of a public bar, near to a log fire and with a pint of beer always in reach.

Card games, billiards, skittles, tiddlywinks, shove ha'penny—all found a permanent place in the

141

British pub and still are a source of keen but friendly rivalry in inter-pub contests.

There is less interest in these games in homes where all eyes are glued to the television set. But a visit to any one of the quaint old pubs of Britain will quickly reveal that dice, dominoes, darts and billiards have lost none of their popularity.

DARTS

The universally popular game of darts is believed to have originated in the English Inns. It is suggested that the game and the dart-board derive from home-made darts thrown at the circular bottoms of beer darrels. In Britain to-day many 'locals' have a darts team, and both friendly matches and organised competitions are played. Rules vary slightly according to the house in which the game is being played, and it is generally accepted that a visitor follows the rules of that particular house.

The dart itself can be of almost any material, shape or size, but the most efficient type has a sharpened steel point, a barrel to give a good finger grip and a feather (or moulded plastic flight). The standard darts board is one having 20 sections formed by dividing wires and each section is numbered, 1 to 20. The bull's-eye is situated in the centre of the board and consists of two concentric circles. The doubles ring is a narrow, wired ring bordering the outer aspect of the 20 sections, while the trebles ring is a concentric ring situated between the bull's-eye and the doubles ring. (See fig. 8).

The dartboard should be placed so that the

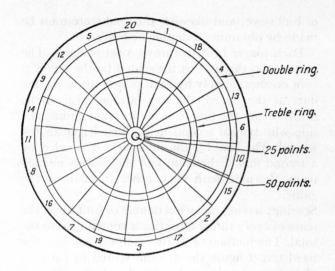

Darts board (Fig. 8)

bull's-eye is a distance of 5 ft. 8 in. from the floor.
A set which consists of 3 darts in all, is thrown
from a toe line 8 to 9 ft. distant from the board.

The Game

A full game consists of 3 'legs' or contests, the
best of three winning the game. Doubles or singles
may be played. In the former, a pair of players
combine their scores, aiming at a total of 501 which
is the usual score for a doubles game. In a singles
game the total required is usually 301.

In either doubles or singles, scoring cannot
commence until a dart lands in the doubles ring

or bull's-eye; and likewise, the final score must be made by obtaining a double or bull's-eye.

Each player in turn throws a set of darts. The player who throws first is decided by the toss of a coin or alternatively by each player throwing one dart at the board, the one landing nearest the centre being the one to lead. In team games, the side who played second in the first leg leads the second. The lead for the third 'leg' is decided by a second toss of the coin, and the players in each team alternate with each other throughout the game.

Scoring: having thrown a double or bull's-eye, the score of every throw after this is contributed to the total. The method of scoring is to deduct from the fixed target figure the amount scored by each set of darts, so the player about to throw always knows the score required to win.

Ask a non-player to volunteer to score, announcing each player's score and recording it with chalk on the board which usually adjoins the dartboard. Scoring darts are those whose points are actually stuck in the board when all three darts have been thrown. Any dart falling from the board in the course of play, or any dart piercing another already in the board does not score.

Second attempts are not permissible. A dart entering the doubles ring scores twice the number of points for that particular section; treble if in the trebles ring. The inner ring of the bull's-eye scores 50, the outer ring 25.

The winning score: this must be a double or bull's-eye. If the agreed total is exceeded, the player has 'bust', no score is awarded and the amount he requires is regarded as still outstanding. Also, should a player require to score only one point, his total remains as it was in his previous score, since 'I' cannot be obtained with a double.

Hints on How to Play Darts

Most players find that the dart is best held between the thumb on the underside and first and second fingers above, and be so balanced. It is then raised to eye level and at the side of the face, the upper arm being kept steady but the wrist loose.

The position of the body should be just slightly right-side-on to the board if right-handed, the body weight being evenly distributed on both feet, the right foot to the toe line but not beyond.

The arm holding the dart is swung back from the elbow and the dart is then thrown forward. The movement should be smooth, yet forceful without jerkiness, taking careful aim of the target. Regular practice is the main key to success.

The high and very low numbers are the most useful in a game, so skill in obtaining these is the first knack to acquire. It is also useful to practice working out how best to divide different final scores, so leaving an even number to be scored by a double in each case.

See that your darts are in good condition, i.e. well flighted, with sharp points which will stick firmly in the board.

Variations on the Basic Darts Game

Cricket

Any even number of players may take part, and are divided into two teams. A coin is tossed to decide whose innings it will be, but the winners may choose to 'bat' or 'bowl'.

The first player of the batting side throws first and aims to score as many points as possible. He is then followed by the first player of the bowling side who aims at bull's-eye; when this has been hit, a wicket has fallen. When 5th wicket has fallen, the teams change over. The game usually concludes when the second set of 5 wickets have fallen, the team having obtained the most 'runs' being the winners.

Football

This game is for two players. Each in turn aims to hit the bull's-eye. The first to do so then aims for doubles, each double scoring a goal. The opponent continues to aim for a bull's-eye until he is successful, then he too aims for goals (doubles). The first player now concentrates on 'recovering the ball'. To do this he must score another bull's-eye and meanwhile cannot score 'goals'.

A game usually consists of 10 goals, the first to obtain this total being the winner.

Round the Clock, or Round the Board

A game for any number of players, each playing individually. A set of darts is thrown by each player and each must obtain a double to commence the game. The aim then is to get a dart into each segment 1–20, and in order. A bull's-eye must then be scored, concluding with a treble.

Should the last dart of the set thrown make a score, this enables the player to have a further 'turn' right away. Apart from this, all players are allowed an equal number of 'throws'. If, for instance, the fifth player is the first to finish, subsequent players may throw, so completing a circuit.

Scram

This is a game for two players. One is a 'stopper', the other a 'scorer'. The 'stopper' throws first and aims to block the scorer; any section into which his darts fall are closed to the 'scorer'. The scorer then throws and aims to score as many as possible in the remaining sections. When all sections are closed, the players change rôles. The player who obtains the highest score is the winner.

Shanghai

Any number may play, each throwing in turn and so progressing round the board. On the first round the first section is aimed for, the second round the second section, and so on round the board. In each round, players attempt to score as many as possible in that particular section; any darts which fall outside that section do not score. If a player fails to score, he nevertheless proceeds to the next section in the next round. The game is won by the player who has the highest aggregate score throughout the game.

Shove Ha'penny

This game is an adaption of the true board game. Any even number may play, usually 2 or 4: one opposes one, or two oppose two.

Each player in turn throws a set of darts aiming them at each of the sections from 1 to 9. Three scores must be made from each of the 9 sections, though any order is permissible. In scoring, a double counts as 2 and trebles equal 3.

Should a player exceed the number of scores required, those in excess are credited to the opposing player(s). The final throw required to win must be scored and cannot be obtained from an opponent.

DOMINOES

Dominoes was introduced into England in the latter part of the 18th century by French prisoners of war. Before reaching England, it was played in France and Italy about the mid-18th century. Dominoes have been played in China for as long as card games.

Today dominoes is a particularly popular game in pubs in the North of England. There are several variations of the game, of which 'threes and fives' is the best known. The value of the domino is reckoned by the number of indented spots on one half, or both halves, and ranges from double blank to double six.

Basic Dominoes

Each player aims to play all his dominoes (this is termed a 'chalk'), and the first to do so wins the chalk. An odd number of chalks decided on by the players constitutes a game; the player who gains the highest number wins the game.

The dominoes are placed face downwards on the table and are shuffled about. Each player then turns up a domino.

The one with the domino of highest spot-value starts the game, and is known as the 'downer'. The upturned dominoes are replaced and all are re-shuffled. Each player then draws an equal number of pieces from the set, according to the number taking part, e.g. four players would have 7 each; 5 players would have five each with three left over. Dominoes remaining are not included in that particular chalk.

Order of play is clockwise from the 'downer'. Also in this order, each player becomes downer in turn. All dominoes including those left over, are shuffled between each chalk.

The downer selects a domino from his hand and places it face upwards in the centre of the table. The next player then plays a domino equal in spot-value to one half or the other of that played by the downer. Dominoes are thus placed end to end, except the doubles, which are placed horizontally. The two extreme ends of the line of dominoes are those to be matched. Should a player at any time be unable to add to the line of played dominoes he raps on the table, so renouncing his turn; but he remains in the game, playing when it is his turn and when he is able to do so.

A chalk is blocked when no player is able to play, whereupon each player shows the dominoes remaining in his hand, counting the total number of spots he holds. The player having the least number of spots wins the chalk. Should two players tie, the chalk is drawn and no score made, in which case the same downer starts the next game.

On playing out all his dominoes, that player calls 'Domino' and so wins the chalk. If this is called wrongly, the player is penalised by each of the players being awarded the score and the chalk then ends. A player may also claim a chalk against another player who renounces wrongly, or who placed a domino which does not match, providing it is detected before the next move.

Variations of the Basic Game

Bergan

A game for two players, each holding a hand of 6 dominoes. The player holding the highest double starts the game. Thereafter, the object is to play dominoes so that a domino bearing the same number of spots is at each end of the row. Each time a player succeeds in obtaining this combination, he scores two points. When a player is unable to play from his hand, he may draw a further piece from the remaining dominoes and play it immediately, if it fits.

The first one to play out all his dominoes adds a further point to his score. Should neither player be able to play, hands are revealed and counted. A player not holding a double scores one point. If both or neither hold a double, all the spots are counted, the player with the lowest number scoring one point. 15 points usually constitute a game.

Bingo

Based on the card game Bezique, this is for two players. The lead is decided and then each player draws a hand of 7 dominoes. The player not leading turns up one of the remaining dominoes and if one half shows more spots than the other then this is the number to be considered as 'trumps'. A blank counts 7.

The first player leads as he chooses, but the second player plays to take the 'trick'. To do this he must play a domino of higher value, or a trump.

The winner of the trick draws a domino from those remaining and leads, after which his opponent draws and plays a domino. This continues until all the dominoes have been drawn.

From this stage onward the second player must follow suit if possible, by matching the domino which has been led. If he is not able to do so he may either play a trump or discard. The winner of the trick counts the score it contains as follows:

A double scores its spot value, a double blank equals 14 (bingo); 6 and 4, and blank and 3 equal 10; all trumps score their spot value, but double trump equals 28. No other pieces carry any score value.

A player having two doubles in his hand may lead one and announce the other, and if he takes the trick he scores 20. Should he hold 3 doubles and win the trick he scores 40; if 4 doubles, 50, and so on. Seven doubles, however, claim 3 points towards game. A game equals 7 up, and 70 points scored in play count one towards game.

Having won a trick, a player who believes he has

a hand which will gain 70 points may turn down the original trump and so end any further drawing of dominoes. Should he subsequently fail to make the seventy points as declared his opponent is awarded 2 points towards game. If the declaration was made before a trick was taken, and the declarer fails, his opponent gains 3 points towards game.

A double blank may take any piece, even a trump; and if it takes double trump the player scores a point.

Block Game

2 or 4 players take part and the basic game of dominoes is played. At the end of a chalk or when the chalk has become blocked, each player counts up the spots on the dominoes he holds. The one with the lowest amount scores the sum total of all the hands, and the first player to reach 100 wins the game.

Domino Pool

This game is very similar to the Block Game. 2 or more players may take part. Each has a hand of 5 dominoes and the basic game is played.

The one holding the highest domino leads. When a chalk is completed, or all are blocked, each player counts the spots on the dominoes he holds and that amount is recorded against him. On reaching 100 he is out of the game, the winner being the last player remaining in the game.

Outdoor skittles

Beer and Dominoes in an Essex Inn
Snooker

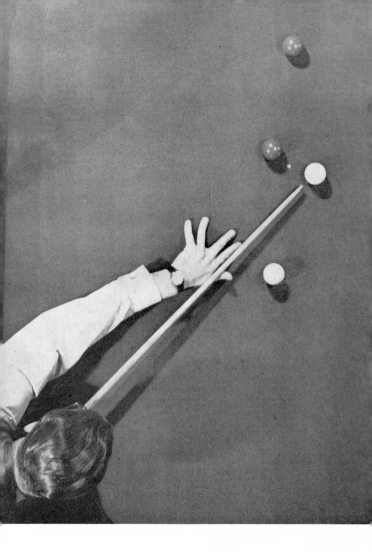

Snooker – the correct bridge of the hand

Laying out a hand in patience
An 'angled shot' in Tuppenny Ha'penny Football
Tiddlywinks are popular in the home and in the pub

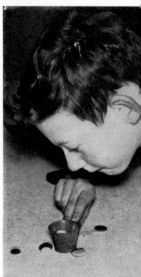

Doubles

4 players take part, each drawing an equal number of dominoes up to 7. The player holding the highest double leads, and following players try to match both ends of the double. After this no further match may be made until the next appropriate double has been played.

On becoming blocked, a player must draw from any remaining dominoes. The winner is the first to play out all his dominoes.

Draw Game

This is for 2 or 4 players and is similar to the Block Game. When a player becomes blocked he may, or may not, draw the remaining dominoes, as he prefers; but any domino he does draw cannot be played until his next turn, or when suitable thereafter.

Another version is to continue drawing until a domino *can* be played. 2 dominoes must remain undrawn.

Fives

This is a game for 2 to 4 players, each having a hand of 7 dominoes. The object is to play the dominoes so that the ends total 5 or multiples of 5. For each '5', one point is scored. Game equals 31 points.

Five and Threes

This is similar to Fives except that 3's, 5's and their multiples score points.

Matador

This game is for 2 players, each of whom draws a hand of 7 dominoes. The dominoes are so played that the open ends of the row will each score 7, or a multiple of 7, for which one point is scored. Before playing a domino a player *may* draw one from those remaining; if blocked, he must do so. 2 dominoes must remain undrawn. The Matadors are 6–1, 5–2, 4–3 and 0–0 and they may be played at any time without having to match. When played they score one point. Game equals 100 points.

Cribbage

Cribbage is the card game most commonly seen in play in pubs. It is fully described on p. 199.

BILLIARDS

No one country can claim the invention of Billiards, but there are references to the game in English literature of the seventeenth century. It was not until the early nineteenth century that the modern code of play was created and then the game gained great popularity, being played extensively in pubs. In modern times, however, it takes second place in popularity to snooker, or pool (in the U.S.A.).

Billiards is played on an eight-legged table with six netted pockets, using three balls and a cue.

The Balls

Of the three balls, two are white and the third is red. They must be equal in size and weight. One of the white balls is marked with two black spots opposite each other, and this is called the 'spot ball' or simply 'spot'. The other white ball is known as 'the plain'.

The Cue

Most cues are about 4 ft. 10 in. long, the only limitation being that they must not be less than 3 ft. in length. The cue is usually made of ash, and it tapers from the thick butt end (held in the hand) to the striking end which is covered with a leather tip.

The Table

The table is made of a slate bed (measuring 12 ft. × 6 ft. 1½ in.) covered with a green woollen cloth.

The bed is within a sturdy wooden frame, all of which is supported by eight wooden legs, the table being 2 ft. 9½ in. to 2 ft. 10½ in. from the ground.

There are six netted pockets (large enough to receive the balls), one at each corner, and one in the middle of each long side of the table. Running along the borders of the table, and between the pockets, are rubber cushions from which the balls re-bound.

Table Markings

A 'baulk line' is drawn 29 in. from, and parallel to, the bottom cushion, and the area between the line and the cushion is known as 'baulk'.

At the centre of the 'baulk' line, a semi-circle is drawn, within the baulk, with an 11½ in.

radius. This semi-circle is the 'D'. A player must make his shot from within the 'D' when he is 'in hand'—that is to say, when his ball is off the table, either because the game has yet to start, or because his ball has dropped into a pocket.

The remaining markings take the form of four spots, all on an imaginary line running up the middle of the playing area. These are:

(1) at the centre of the 'D' semi-circle.
(2) at the centre of the table; this spot is known as the 'centre spot'.
(3) at a point halfway between the centre spot and the top cushion, known as the 'pyramid spot'.
(4) at a point $12^3/_4$ in. from the top cushion, known as the 'billiard spot'.

The object of the game is to score more points than one's opponent, there being usually only two players competing. The cue ball must be hit with the cue-tip. Points are scored in three different ways:

(1) *The Cannon*

This is scored when a player strikes his ball (known as the cue-ball) in such a way that it hits the other two balls, that is, his opponent's white (known as the 'object white') and the red. The Cannon is worth two points.

(2) *The Winning Hazard* (also known as the 'pot').

This is scored when the player strikes his cue-ball in such a way that it hits one of the other object balls, causing it to enter the pocket. Potting the white is worth two points. Potting the red is worth three points.

(3) *The Losing Hazard* (also known as the 'loser', or 'in-off')

This is scored when the player hits his cue-ball in such a way that it hits one of the other two balls and then enters a pocket. A 'loser' off the object white scores two points. A 'loser' off the red scores three points.

A game is usually ended (a) when a player reaches a given number of points (100, 250, 500, etc.) or (b) at the end of an agreed period of time. In this case, the player with the greater number of points is declared the winner.

The foregoing is necessarily only a digest of the complete rules of billiards, intended only as a short guide. The complete rules (including fouls, types of shots, types of play, etc.) can be obtained from the Billiards Association and Control Council.

SNOOKER

Though snooker arrived on the scene much later than billiards, it is today the more popular game. Snooker is a 'potting' game, though it has rather more refinements than 'pool', its American cousin.

Four handed snooker is very popular.

The table used for snooker is identical to that used for billiards. The cues are also the same. (See fig. 9).

Twenty-two balls are used in snooker. These are:

The cue ball (white) which each player uses in turn.

Red balls. There are 15 of these.

Coloured balls (also known as pool balls) of which

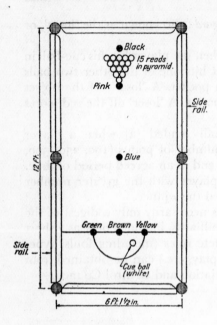

Labels within figure: Black, 15 reads in pyramid., Pink, Side rail., Blue, Green Brown Yellow, Side rail., Cue ball (white), 12 Ft., 6 Ft. 1½ in.

Snooker table (Fig. 9)

there are six: yellow, green, brown, blue, pink and black.

Position of the Balls

The fifteen red balls are formed into a pyramidal pack, the top red, at the apex, being as close as possible to, though not actually touching, the pink. The pink is on 'pyramid spot', the black is behind the pack on the 'billiard spot', the blue is on the centre spot.

The green, brown and yellow are on the baulk

line, the green on the left hand extremity of the 'D' semi-circle, the brown in the centre, and the yellow on the right hand extremity of the 'D'.

Snooker offers only one method of scoring, and that is the winning hazard. As we have said, snooker is a 'potting' game, but it also provides a method of obstructing your opponent. This is by 'snookering'.

The object of the game is to pot all the balls (excluding the white) in the following sequence: first, a red; second, any colour the player nominates; third, a red; fourth, any colour the player nominates… and so on until all 15 reds have been potted. Colours are returned to their original spot each time they are potted, but when a red has been potted it is left in the pocket.

When all the reds have been cleared, the colours must be potted in the following sequence: yellow, green, brown, blue, pink and black. At this stage, colours remain in the pockets in which they are potted.

A player continues in this sequence until he fails to pot a ball. His opponent then takes over.

Scoring

Points are scored as follows: potting a red equals 1 point; yellow equals 2 points; green equals 3 points; brown equals 4 points; blue equals 5 points; pink equals 6 points; black equals 7 points.

Points obtained in sequence are added together and the total obtained before the sequence ends is known as the 'break'.

The winner of the game is the player with the

most points when the game ends, and the game ends when black only remains and is potted.

Each game is known as a 'frame' and a match is composed of a given number of frames.

Snookering

A player is 'snookered' when he is prevented from hitting the 'on' ball (the one to be struck next) by a direct shot with his cue-ball. To get out of a snooker, the player is usually obliged to play his cue-ball off the cushion in the hope that it will rebound and strike the 'on' ball before it strikes any other ball.

Should the player completely miss the 'on' ball, or hit a ball which is not 'on', then he is penalised according to the value of the ball concerned.

Again the above is necessarily only a brief summary of the complete rules of Snooker which can be obtained from the Billiards Association and Control Council.

SHOVE HA'PENNY

This game was a popular pastime in the reign of King Henry VIII but its earliest origin is not known. Today the game remains popular especially in pubs in the South of England.

A Shove-ha'penny board is made of slate, marble or hardwood (if of hardwood the grain should run lengthwise), and measures 2 ft. × 14½ in. Ten lines spaced at 1¼ in. intervals are drawn across the board, so making nine beds, and 1¼ in. from each long side of the board are drawn two more parallel lines. These indicate the boundaries of

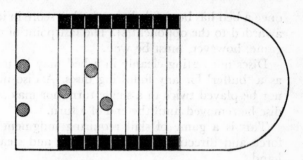

Shove ha'penny (Fig. 10)

play and the spaces outside these lines are used for recording scores. Parallel to the bottom edge and 1½ in. in, is screwed a batten which prevents movement of the board during play. (See fig. 10).

Two individuals or two pairs may play. Metal discs are used, 5 in all, each the size of a halfpenny. The object of the game is to strike the discs so that they come to rest cleanly in the beds. Discs left touching a line do not score, and a disc sent beyond the farthermost line is considered to be out of play. A game, which consists of scoring 3 times in each bed, is termed a 'horse', and a match is the best of 3 horses.

Order of play is decided by tossing a coin. The player who starts places his first disc so that it overlaps slightly the lower edge of the board, and then he strikes it either with the flat of his palm, or the ball of his thumb in order to send it up the board. All five discs are dispatched in a similar manner. The beds may be filled in any order, but once a bed has been filled, any further score in it is awarded to the opponent(s). The last point of the game, however, must be won.

Discs not resting cleanly in a bed may be used as a 'buffer' for any following discs. A disc may nor be played twice in a single turn, nor may any disc be removed until the end of a turn.

This is a game of skill requiring judgment of force and direction, an accurate eye and steady hand.

SKITTLES

This requires a special room, and so today in Britain it is confined to pubs in certain communities in which it is regarded as a traditional pastime. Skittles was introduced into England from the Continent in the 14th century. It has since taken many different forms. Dutch settlers introduced the game into the U.S.A. as ninepins, and recently it has returned to Britain in a modern, streamlined form as the sport of Tenpin Bowling. But the original version still persists, and indeed is gaining in popularity in some English pubs.

For the pub game the skittles stand on a hornbeam frame which is 4 ft. 6 in. square. Nine skittles each not more than 14½ in. high, and 6¾ in. wide at the thickest part and 3 in. at base are positioned on circular metal plates in a diamond pattern with one skittle in the centre.

3 balls or cheeses (which are circular flat discs) are pitched by each player. 2 to 24 players may take part. Each skittle knocked down scores 1 point. A throw of 3 cheeses is a 'chalk' and 3 chalks a 'leg'.

The player, or team with the highest score, wins the leg and a match is the best of 3 legs.

When playing the thrower must have one heel at least 21 ft. from the frame. He may advance one step before the cheese leaves his hand, but must not advance beyond a line 15½ ft. distant from the frame until the cheese has become dead, i.e. when it is motionless and there is no movement of skittles.

It is possible to knock down all 9 pins with one cheese, whereupon they are again setup. A cheese which touches the back or side of the alley, after or before passing through the frame, is ruled 'foul' and must be instantly removed. Also a dead cheese or any pins touched by a foul cheese, must be replaced. A special scoring system is used for games played under the rules of the Amateur Skittle Association.

TIDDLYWINKS

Inter-pub competitions and charity tournaments have taken the well-known party game of Tiddly-winks out of the homes and into the pubs of England.

It has always been a game of skill and accurate judgment, for the art of flicking a disc into a bowl is by no means as simple as it might sound. Pub teams fight 'tooth and nail' against their opponents, encouraged by the cheers of their supporters and no doubt by the usual reward of a free pint for the winners.

Tiddlywinks is played on the ground or on a table. The bowl is placed in the centre, and the players (two-a-side, four-a-side, or all-against-all) form round it, each having six tiddlywink discs of one distinctive colour, and a larger 'flicking disc'. The aim is to get all six small discs into the centre bowl before one's opponents can do so.

Discs are propelled towards the cup in hopping movements achieved by pressing down the larger 'flicking disc' on to the surface edge of a smaller.

Players take it in turns to flick one disc, and should a disc go directly into the bowl the successful player is allowed an extra turn. If he misses, then on his next turn he must flick the disc from wherever it is now situated. Players need not concentrate on the same disc with every turn. Often a player's aim will be to get all his discs into the centre near the bowl and then to concentrate on holing them one by one.

If a disc is covered by an opponent's, the owner must leave it and continue with another, or miss his turn if the covered disc happens to be his last unholed one.

CARD GAMES

We probably have to thank Charles VI of France for the invention of playing cards. When, in 1391, he showed the first signs of the illness which eventually took him to his grave, a game was invented to help cheer him up which used a pack of cards very similar to those we know today.

However, the history books disagree about the origins of playing cards. Their invention is attributed to the Romans, the gypsies, the Italians and the Spanish; but there is no real evidence to show that cards were in existence in Europe earlier than the fourteenth century. These earliest known playing cards—'Tarats'—contained 62, 78 and 97 in a pack and were quite different from our modern version. They derived either from ancient drawings on Oriental tablets of stone or from the chess game, and quickly spread all over the world, being imported to England from France in the fifteenth century and taken by merchants and sailors to all the major ports.

We have included a few of the most popular games, grouped according to the type of game.

Bridge

Bridge in all its various forms developed from the game of whist which dates back about 400 years. Auction Bridge developed at the beginning of the 20th century, followed approximately twenty years later by a further development, Contract Bridge. The latter is the most popular form in the present day, being played casually or formally, in the home, or in clubs and in tournaments. The game is deeply rewarding for those who wish to master its complexity yet also can be enjoyed by those not wishing to take it so seriously.

There are other types of bridge, for example, Honeymoon, Progressive and Three-handed, and also other varying methods of play. Many books have been written on this game, but the most satisfactory method of learning is to play as frequently as possible. Outlined here is the basic game.

Contract Bridge

There are two main types of Contract Bridge: Rubber Bridge, which is played widely in the home and at clubs throughout the country, and Competitive Bridge, which, although played to the same basic rules, calls for a vastly different technique.

The beginner should concentrate upon Rubber Bridge, and this is played by four players, in two sets of partners, using one pack of 52 cards.

Suits rank as: Spades high, Hearts, Diamonds, Clubs, with, additionally, a 'no trumps' call which ranks above Spades.

The cards rank: Ace high to deuce low.

The players cut for partners, with the two highest opposing the two lowest. The player cutting the highest card has the choice of seats, his partner sitting opposite. Highest card has the deal, the 52 cards being dealt singly, in a clockwise manner, until each player has 13 cards.

It is usual to use two packs of cards, a pack being used for alternate deals. The packs should have two different colour backs, the original dealer having choice of colour. The deal rotates to the left, so that after four hands, each player has dealt.

Following the deal, each player assesses his hand and must make a 'call'. The dealer has the first call, which must either be a 'bid' or a pass. If a player wishes to pass, he must call 'no bid'. Should he wish to make a bid, then there are a great number of variations open to him.

Skilful calling and correct interpretation of calls between partners, is a vital factor of the game.

A bid: The lowest possible call is 'one club', which means that a player making this bid contracts to make seven tricks, with clubs as trumps. In effect, a call of 'one' means that the player contracts to make one more than six, for obviously, if one pair make seven tricks the other pair must have made six, thus one more than six.

Assuming an opening bid of one club, next player has the choice of either saying 'no bid', 'double' or of making a higher bid. According to the style being used, 'double' means that the player is either asking his partner to call his best suit, and is thus known as a 'take out double' or else he is telling his partner that he feels that they can beat one club. If he makes a higher bid, this can be as low as 'one diamond', for at Contract Bridge a higher ranking suit can be bid at the same level.

Thus it is quite possible for an Auction, as the calling is called, to start in this manner. For convenience we will call the original dealer 'North' and his partner 'South', whilst the opponents are known as 'East' (the player sitting on the original caller's left) and 'West'. Thus: North – one club; East – one diamond; South – one heart; West – one spade; North – one no trumps.

When three players in succession have said 'no bid', the Auction closes and the side which has made the highest bid will play the hand. The hand is played, not necessarily by the last player to have made a call, but by the player who first called the suit (or no trumps) in which the hand is to be played. Thus, to return to the Auction shown above, if it continued: East – no bid; South – three no trumps, and then the next three players say 'no bid', the hand would be played by North, who first called no trumps, and not South, who actually made the last positive bid. North is now known as the Declarer, and East, on his left, will make the first lead.

As soon as East has led—he may choose any card

in his hand—South becomes 'Dummy' and lays all his cards upon the table. If the hand is being played in a trump suit, this suit must be laid on the right. The Dummy hand is now played by the Declarer. Dummy, however, has certain rights. He may, for example, say 'no diamonds, partner' if on the lead of a diamond by another player, he plays another suit when it comes to his turn.

It is important, at this stage, to understand that at Contract Bridge all calls or statements have to be made using an exact wording. Thus 'no bid', 'one club', or 'no diamonds, partner', must not be varied in any way. This is particularly important at Tournament Bridge. One pair entering a well known tournament were found to open every hand with the bid of one club. However, instead of using the accepted form of 'one club', their calling ranged from 'one club', through 'one club, partner', up to 'I bid one club'. It was found that they had a partnership understanding, and thus every variation of call had a different meaning to them! Naturally, they were expelled from the tournament. It should also be noted that all calls should be made with a voice of the same expression, and that no gestures should be used to convey pleasure or displeasure at either partner's, or an opponent's call.

To return to our mythical deal: after all four players have played a card, the highest card of the suit originally led on that round takes the trick, and the player taking the trick makes the next lead, which may be any card remaining in his hand. This system proceeds until all thirteen tricks have been completed, when, should North have made nine tricks or more, he will have fulfilled his contract of 'three no trumps'. The only variation to this is if the final contract is in a suit, say 'four hearts'. If a player is unable to play a card of the suit led he may play a trump (or of course he may throw away another suit). In a suit contract, the highest trump played in the round wins the trick, or if no trump has been played then, as before, the highest card of the suit originally led.

It will be seen that no less than 35 positive bids can be made, ranging from 'one club' to 'seven no trumps'. In addition, other permissible calls are 'double' or 're-double'. 'Double' has already been explained, and the call can be used at any stage of the Auction, but only by the opponents of the side last making a positive bid. Thus it is impossible to double your own partner's call.

'Re-double' can be used only after the call 'double', and can be made only by either of the opponents of the side having called 'double'. There are two main uses of this call. In one case, it is used when the side expecting to become Declarers consider that they will make their call. Thus, if North bids three diamonds, and East doubles, South may well re-double if he feels that North and he may make nine tricks with diamonds as trumps. This call is widely made at a low level. For example if North opens one diamond and East doubles, a re-double by South would tell North that South has a fair hand with diamond support. In this event either West or East will almost certainly make a bid. West, for example, may well bid one spade if he has a good spade suit. He knows that East would not have doubled unless he held a useful hand, and even if his only honour card was, say, the king of spades, if he held six spades and only one diamond, he could well expect to take a considerable number of tricks, for he can expect his partner to hold at least three spades. If partner had held an unbalanced hand with, say, six hearts and few spades, he would have bid hearts, and not doubled.

The other widely used occasion when 're-double' is called is when the player making this call wishes to inform his partner that he feels that the contract would be a disaster, and invites his partner to call another suit. To take an easy example: North bids one diamond, East one heart, South no bid, West two clubs, North two diamonds, East double. If South now says 're-double' he is telling his partner that he will be no help at all to him in a diamond contract, otherwise he would have been able to bid originally over East's one heart. There is also a strong inference that South would welcome a spade call. Of course, he could call 'two spades' himself, but by re-doubling he gives North a chance to make the decision. Imagine the strained feelings afterwards if North is found to have nine diamonds and no spades, and could have made two diamonds, whereas poor South only makes five tricks with spades as trumps instead of eight!

Conventions: it will be obvious that with calls having so many meanings, to form a successful partnership one must understand what each call is intended to mean. But it is considered unfair for a partnership to make calls which have a special meaning to them, which is hidden from their opponents. Therefore, before any game commences, each side must inform the other which conventions they are playing. All conventions have to be recognised by the COMMITTEE OF THE PORTLAND CLUB. Therefore groups of conventions and styles have become accepted and are known as systems. If you play at a club, you may well be told by your opponents that they are playing the 'Two Club' system, which is widely used in club play. 'Acol' is another system extensively used, especially by tournament and other better players, whilst, as you progress, you are likely to hear of 'Vienna', 'C. A. B.', 'the Barton Club', 'Culbertson', and many others.

Unfortunately, the game has become somewhat over systemised, and if you went along to a tournament and sat behind well known players, you might be forgiven if you thought that you were listening to a foreign language if they informed their opponents that they were playing 'Acol with the weak no trump, Herbert, Gerber, Flint Transfer, Grand Slam Force and revolving discards'! The purpose of this book is not to explain these systems, but the keen player will soon pick up a working knowledge of the better known systems and conventions, and there are many excellent books published by leading players should you be really keen.

The main object of Contract Bridge is to score a game, which is 100 points, three games constituting a rubber, as will be seen in the appendage. Three no trumps, four spades or four hearts, five diamonds or five clubs are all final contracts which will score a game outright. Often, however, the hand is played in a lower contract. If you bid and make, say, two hearts, you will score 60 points towards game, and this is known as a part score. Often, when both sides have a part score, bidding becomes very competitive.

To take an extreme case, if both sides have a score of 90, even one club (scoring 20 points) bid and made would give a side a game. Opponents are unlikely to let you play at this low level, and there are often opportunities for doubling after the bidding has reached too high a level.

Scoring: this takes place when the cards have been played out. Each side has a 'Trick Score' and a 'Premium Score'. (1) Trick Score: This is the point value of odd tricks as contracted, i.e. if the declarer made the tricks as bid that amount is credited to the trick score, or 'below the line'. (2) Premium Score: This consists of scores credited for (a) Tricks made in excess of the bid. (b) Honours held in one hand. (c) Bid and made slams. (d) Winning a rubber. (e) Under tricks. (This is called 'above the line'). Should a declarer fail to make his contract the defenders score a premium amount for each trick by which he failed.

Twelve tricks is a 'little slam'; thirteen odd tricks is a 'grand slam'. If such are bid and made a premium is gained. Game consists of 100 trick points. Two games won by one side equals one rubber. After a partnership winning a game both sides then again commence their trick scores from zero.

Vulnerability: This is when a side has won the first game of a rubber. Premium for excess tricks in contracts doubled or redoubled and for slams are increased, but so, too, are the penalties for under tricks.

Honours: These are the Ace, King, Queen, Jack, and Ten of the trump suit. Any player holding four or all of these cards receives a premium. This applies also to a player holding all four Aces in a no-trump contract.

Winning the rubber scores a premium of 700 points if the other side have not won again, otherwise the score is 500 points. The trick scores and premium scores are then totalled, the side having most points having won the rubber.

TABLE OF CONTRACT BRIDGE SCORES:

Odd tricks won as bid:

Clubs and Diamonds: 20 each trick; 40 doubled; 80 redoubled.

Hearts and Spades: 30 each trick; 60 doubled; 120 redoubled.

No trumps, 1st trick: 40; 80 doubled; 160 redoubled.

No trumps following tricks: 30; 60 doubled; 120 redoubled.

Overtricks

Each undoubled trick scores its value as above.

Each doubled: 100 not vulnerable; 200 vulnerable.

Each redoubled: 200 not vulnerable; 400 vulnerable.

Making a doubled or redoubled contract: 50 points.

Undertricks

Each such undoubled trick scores for the defenders: 50 not vulnerable; 100 vulnerable.

Doubled

1st trick: 100 not vulnerable; 200 vulnerable.
Following tricks: 200 not vulnerable; 300 vulnerable.

Redoubled

1st trick: 200 not vulnerable; 400 vulnerable.
Following tricks: 400 not vulnerable; 600 vulnerable.

Honours

All in a trump bid or four Aces in a no-trump bid: 150 points.
Four trump cards in a trump contract: 100 points.
Little slam bid and won: 500 not vulnerable; 750 vulnerable.
Grand slam bid and won: 1000 not vulnerable; 1500 vulnerable.

Rubber Points

Three game rubber: 500 points.
Two game rubber: 700 points.
One game of an unfinished rubber: 300 points.

Auction Bridge

This is similar to Contract Bridge, the main

difference being in the scoring as here outlined:

For bids won as declared each trick scores as follows:

	Undoubled	Doubled	Redoubled
No Trumps	10	20	40
Spades	9	18	36
Hearts	8	16	32
Diamonds	7	14	28
Clubs	6	12	24

30 + points scored for odd tricks wins one game, and the next game is begun. A rubber is won when a side wins two games, for which 250 points are added to their score.

For a doubled contract made, a bonus of 50 points is scored plus 50 points for each over trick. If a re-doubled contract is made then the bonus is 100 points plus 100 points for each over-trick. Although these bonuses are added to the trick score they do not count towards game.

For a contract not made each under trick scores 50 points to the opponents, 100 points if a doubled contract, and 200 if re-doubled.

Honours scores: Three honours or Aces equal 30, four honours or Aces divided equal 40, five honours divided equal 50, four trump honours in one hand equal 80, four trump honours in one hand, fifth in partner's hand equal 90, four Aces in one hand when no-trumps equal 100, five honours in one hand equal 100.

Little slam: a side winning twelve tricks irrespective of contract equals 50; grand slam is all thirteen tricks irrespective of contract and equals 100 points. Odd tricks only count towards game as fulfilment of contract.

Hints: the skill in playing bridge is in the bidding. In general, the first bids are under calls, but serve to combine the possibilities within two partner's hands. In play it is wise to play trumps first when declared, then strong suits. A defender's lead should be the highest held in that suit first called by his partner, and before leading his strongest suit the partner's lead should be returned.

Bezique

There are various forms of this game, such as six and eight pack Bezique and Rubicon and adaptations for three and four hand games. Outlined here, however, is the basic game for two players. Two packs of 32 cards shuffled together are used, deuce to six inclusive of each suit being removed from each pack. Cards rank Ace high to seven low.

Players cut for deal, which is taken by the lowest card. The cards are dealt eight to each player in the order of three, two, three. The seventeenth card is up-turned to denote the trump suit. The remaining cards become stock and are placed face down between the two players.

The object of the game now is to obtain points from 'Brisques' and specific declarations. (Brisques are tricks including tens and Aces). Playing the cards: initially, the non-dealer leads any card of his choice, and thereafter the tricks winner leads. A trick is won by being trumped, or by the highest ranking card of the suit led. It is not compulsory to follow suit at this stage.

A declaration may be made following the winning of a trick. The declaration cards are placed face up on the table where they remain until again used in play, which the player may do at any time. Although more than one at a time may be made, only one at a time can score (after each trick won). One card may be used in declarations of a different combination, but not twice in the same combination. Example: Four Kings may be declared and one of these four may also be used to declare a marriage. Should yet another King appear in the hand and be added to the remaining three Kings, such a declaration would not be valid as three of the Kings have already been used in such a declaration.

It is permitted to add further to a declaration, forming yet another declaration and adding to the score of the first. Example: Bezique may be declared (scoring 40). Another Bezique may then be added so producing double Bezique and a further 500 is scored, equalling 540 in all. If, however, Double Bezique is declared at one and the same time, the score is 500 only (see table of scores on next page).

Following a trick the winner draws the top stock card, and the opponent the one below it. Play continues thus until the stock is exhausted, whereupon cards exposed are now taken into the hand. The last trick winner leads and in playing these cards, the suit must be followed and a trick taken if able.

Game consists of 1500 or 1000 points. If this total is reached by both players on the same deal, the final higher score wins. Seven of trumps: if this is turned up as trump card, the dealer scores ten points. Also, on winning a trick either player may exchange seven of trumps for the trump card, or seven trumps may be declared (scoring ten).

The above game can be adapted for play by three or four players, in which case an extra 32-card pack per player is required. Game is then 2000. Bezique may be played without a trump, in which case no trump card is turned up and seven trumps score, etc. does not exist. The first declared marriage denotes trump suit.

Bezique Scoring Table

Marriage: King and Queen of same suit	20
Royal Marriage: King and Queen of trumps	40
Sequence: Ace, King, Queen, Jack, Ten of trumps	200
Bezique: Queen Heart, Jack Diamond	40
Double Bezique: Queen Heart, Jack Diamond, Queen Heart, Jack Diamond	500
Four Aces (Any)	100
Four Kings (Any)	80
Four Queens (Any)	60
Four Jacks (Any)	40
Brisque (A trick containing a Ten or Ace) ..	10
Winning last trick	10

Seven trumps 10
(Brisques and last trick won are not counted until
play ends).

Whist

Four players take part with two partners opposing another pair. One pack of 52 cards is used.
In play, the cards rank as Ace high down to deuce,
low.

To determine partners each player cuts or draws
from the pack. The two highest play against the
two lowest. Low card takes the choice of cards and
seats. (In the draw only, Ace counts low). Each
player may shuffle, the dealer doing so last; the
player to the dealer's right cuts. Beginning with
the player to his left, the dealer deals to each player
in a clockwise direction one card at a time, face
down. The last card to be dealt is the trump card,
which is placed face up on the table before the
dealer. The card remains so placed until it is the
dealer's turn to play.

The object of the game is to win tricks. The
player to the dealer's left leads any card of his
choice. Play follows in clockwise direction from
player to player and each player must follow suit
if possible. If unable to follow suit a trump or any
other card may be played. The trick is taken by the
highest trump card. If a trump has not been played,
the trick is taken by the highest card of the suit
led. The player of the winning card then leads and
the game continues thus until all cards have been
played.

Scoring: Five points constitute a game, and the

best of three games a rubber. One point is awarded for each trick beyond six to the winning side. Ace, King, Queen, Jack of trumps are honours and a side holding these scores four points. If they hold three then three points are scored. These points may not be claimed, however, if at the beginning of a deal the players already hold four points. If in a game the losers haven't scored, the winners gain three points. If the losers' score is less than three the winners gain two points, and for a total of three or four to the losers, one point is gained by the winners. Two extra points are awarded the rubber winners. The value of the losers' game is deducted from the winners' score when three games are played.

Revoking: The opponents of the player at fault may take three tricks, add three points to their score or deduct three points from the revoker.

Hints: Lead trumps if five or more are held, otherwise lead from strongest suit held. If holding a sequence, lead highest, then follow with lowest. Win with lowest card possible. Improve your partner's lead if possible, otherwise play low. Remember the cards played and those which opponents may trump.

German Whist

This is a game for two players using a 52-card pack. Each player has thirteen cards. The remainder are placed face down in the centre of the table. The top card is upturned to denote trumps. The non-dealer leads any card of his choice, the opponent following suit if possible. The winner of the trick takes the upturned card, the loser the card below it and then the top card of the pack is upturned. The game proceeds in this manner, until the pack is exhausted. As each trick winner has taken the exposed card, both players at this stage will have some idea what cards are in his opponent's hand. The cards are now played out and the winner is the one with most of the tricks.

Canasta

This game derives from Rummy and originated in South America where it spread and reached the U.S.A. approximately fifteen years ago. The word 'Canasta' is Spanish, meaning 'basket'.

The game may be played by two to six players and there are various methods of play. Described here is the basic game for four players, who play in two partnerships.

Two ordinary packs of cards are used plus four jokers, making 108 cards in all.

The object of the game is to form sets of cards of the same rank consisting of three or more per set (as opposed to Rummy, sequences are not valid).

Wild Cards are the deuces and jokers and when used with other cards, may take their rank.

A Meld is a set of three or more cards of the same rank, which must contain at least two natural cards to be valid and not more than three wild cards.

Canasta: this consists of a set of seven or more cards and must include at least four natural cards. If all the cards are natural, this produces a 'pure' canasta. A 'mixed' canasta contains wild cards.

Red Treys: any player obtaining a red three

must place it face up on the table and draw another card, (unless the red three has been taken with the discard pile, whereupon no replacement draw is made). Each of these cards have a value of 100 points and this amount is credited at the end of play providing melds have been made. If no melds have been made, this amount is debited. If a side has all four red threes, they score a total of 800 points.

Partnership is decided by draw, and the two highest play the two lowest. The highest card drawn has choice of seats and takes the lead in the first hand. Partners sit opposite each other. The deal is taken by the player sitting to the right of the one who drew highest card. Each player is dealt a total of eleven cards in the usual manner. The remainder is the 'stock' and is placed face down in the centre of the table. The top card is now upturned and placed by the stock. Should this card be a wild card or a black or red trey, further cards are upturned until a natural card appears.

Playing the cards: each player in turn draws a card from stock and may make a meld; he also must discard a card which then ends his turn. A player may draw a card from the discard pile providing his side has made its first meld or requires the top card to do so and that the discard pile is not 'frozen'. The first meld must total a minimum amount according to the existing score of the side at that time. The amount is totalled by counting the points value of each card in the meld. To do this, two or more different melds may be made. If this involves taking the discard pile it is permitted to count the top card toward the score (any other bonuses are not valid at this stage). If the side has no score at all the minimum amount required is 15, and if less than 1,495 it is 50. 1500 to 2995 requires 90 and more than 3000 requires 120.

Discard Pile: If a player draws from this pile he must hold in his hand two natural cards, or one natural and one wild card which match the top card of the pile. Before drawing, he must show these particular cards. Drawing from this pile is also permitted if the top card is required to add to melds already formed.

The discard pile is 'frozen' if its top card is a black three, wild card or red three. A player takes the top card of the discard pile legally, and he then adds all the remaining cards of the pile to his hand. The melds of a partnership are set before one of the two players. In turn, a player is allowed to meld as many cards as he chooses, forming new ones or adding to previous ones. Partners may meld a rank already melded by opponents, but are not allowed to make two separate melds of one rank themselves.

Going out: this is when a player plays out the last card in his hand by discarding or melding; play then ends and scores are totalled. A player cannot 'go out', however, unless his side has a canasta or unless his last card completes a canasta; otherwise, he must keep one card in his hand. Holding only one card, he is not permitted to take a discard pile of only one card. A player may ask his partner's permission to 'go out'. The reply may not be more than 'yes' or 'no' and either is binding.

A 'Concealed Hand' is when a player plays out all his cards in one turn, without having previously added to or made any meld, and in so playing out his cards one canasta must be included.

Depletion of stock: if the last card from the stock pile is a red three the player exposes it and may not discard or meld further until play ends. Play continues, however, if the last card is not a red three. In this event the discard must be taken by a player if it matches one of his melds, but need not be taken to form a new meld. When a player in turn cannot take the discard, play ends. A discarded black trey acts as a 'stop' card by preventing the next player in turn from taking the discard pile. A wild card may also be used as a 'stop' card.

Scoring: game is 5,000. The hand in which this score is reached should be played out and the difference between the two final totals is the margin of victory. Each card has its own point value: Joker equals 50; Deuce equals 20; Ace equals 20; King, Queen, Jack, Ten, Nine, Eight equal 10; 7, 6, 5, 4 and Black Trey equal 5; a natural canasta equals 500; mixed canasta equals 300. (The canasta points are in addition to the point values of the cards forming the canasta). When play ends, all cards held in the hand count minus, even though the hand contains a meld, and this amount is deducted from the total point score. Going out—100 points, Going out with a concealed hand—200.

Penalties: (1) Putting down an insufficient count for the initial meld may be corrected by rearranging the meld or adding to it, but if all the cards are retracted the minimum amount for the initial meld is increased by 10 points. (2) Incorrectly melding—100 points debit. (3) Taking the discard pile and not showing valid claim—100 points debit. (4) If receiving permission to go out and then unable to do so—100 points debit.

Hints: The aim is to score points by melding and canastas when possible and the skill lies in knowing how and when to meld and when to go out. The discard pile signifies extra values and obtaining it should be the set objective. Don't discard to give your opponents the discard pile or a canasta, nor break up your own hand. Use the cards or black trey as stop cards to limit your opponents' canastas.

Poker

It is impossible to play poker 'for love'; its main excitement is in winning the stakes, more so when you have outwitted an opponent by inducing him to throw up his hand when, in reality, you have a worse one yourself.

The gambler's delight, Poker is often called the national game of America, although it has become popular the world over. One cannot dwell here at great length on all of its somewhat complicated rules and variations. Perhaps the most popular game is Draw Poker—or, simply, Poker—which is an adaptation of, and an improvement on, the long-established game of Brag.

Up to seven players take part and an ordinary pack of 52 cards is cut to decide the dealer. Each player, dealer included, receives five cards, dealt face down, one at a time, beginning at the dealer's left. Once this has been done, the betting starts.

Player on the dealer's left has the first option to bet. Chips are put into a central kitty (or 'pot' as it is called) by those players who want to come in on the game; the remainder drop out.

The active players now pass into a card-exchange phase (or 'draw' as it is called). They can discard all or any number of their cards and receive, in exchange from the dealer, an equal number of cards, face downward from the top of the main pack.

Players do not have to exchange any cards if they feel their hand is strong enough.

The sole aim is to secure any one of a number of high scoring combinations in the following strictly defined order of value:

Royal Flush: Ace, King, Queen, Jack, Ten of a suit.

Straight Flush: five cards of the same suit sequence.

Fours: four cards of the same denomination.

Full House: three cards of one denomination, two of another.

Flush: all five cards of the same suit, not in sequence.

Straight: five cards in sequence regardless of suit.

Threes: three cards of the same denomination.

Two pairs.

One pair.

Highest card: Ace high.

With similar hands, the highest card wins, e.g. flush Jack high beats flush Ten high; straight to

Queen beats straight to Jack, and so on.

There now comes the serious betting period in which each player stakes a certain number of chips that *his* hand will defeat those of his opponents.

The player whose turn it is to start the betting puts enough chips into the pot to cover his own evaluation of the strength of his hand. Then, in turn, the others may drop out, call the bet (put in the same number of chips) or one may raise the previous bets by putting in a greater number of chips to indicate that his hand is the best hand.

This continues round the table until there is no further raise. Then the player who last bet takes the pot, unless he has been 'seen' or 'called', when he shows his hand, and if it is best he takes the pot. If it is not, then the player who actually does hold the best hand wins.

Of the many variations of basic poker, we have selected the following, as it is thought to be one of the most popular and interesting.

Stud Poker

Any number from two to ten may play, and each is dealt one card face down and one face up. The player with the highest card showing places the first bet, and the betting proceeds, after which the dealer gives those players still in the game another card, face up. After more betting, another card is dealt to each player still in, face up, and so on until each remaining player has five cards.

In each betting round, the player with the highest card or the highest poker combination showing has the first turn to bet. If two or more players tie for highest, the one nearest dealer's left initiates the betting.

Brag

This is the accepted forerunner of Poker and is one of England's oldest card games. Each hand consists of three cards (instead of five as in Poker).

All the cards in a pack are used, but special preference is given to the *ace of diamonds*, *jack of clubs* and *nine of diamonds*. Called the 'braggers', they can stand for any other card.

Having cut for the deal, the winning player puts any stake he wishes into the centre pot (up to an agreed limit) and deals each of the players (himself included) with three cards, face down, starting with the player on his left. Once this is done, betting starts.

Players all look at their cards: the one on the dealer's left may (a) put in at least as much as the original stake to stay in the game, (b) raise the bet (put in a bigger sum indicating his hand is best), or (c) drop out of that round.

Every player coming into the game must, in any event, pay into the pot as much as the highest individual stake; or else he must throw away his hand and lose any money he may already have paid.

If no one will place a bet, the dealer receives an agreed amount from each of the others and the deal passes to the left.

However, should a player stake an amount which no other is prepared to meet, he then takes the pot without showing his hand. Should a call be made, all the hands must be shown and the best brag hand wins.

Bearing in mind that the *ace of diamonds*, *the jack of clubs* and *the nine of diamonds* ('braggers') can stand for any card the holder so decides, the order of value in Brag is:

1. Three Aces (in which no 'bragger' is employed).
2. Three Aces (with the assistance of a 'bragger').
3. Three Kings (or other smaller cards in due order, the higher being preferred to the lower, and as between threes of equal value, 'naturals' being preferred to those made with the help of a 'bragger' card).
4. Pairs (from Aces downwards, in like manner, with the same preference of natural pairs).
5. In default of any pair or better, the hand holding the best single card, the Ace of diamonds ranking first (and after it any other Ace and so on).

Three Stake Brag

This is one of the variations of simple Brag in which each player contributes to three separate stakes, known as the First, Second and Third Stake.

Three cards are then dealt out to each player, two face down and the third face up. The holder of the highest face-up card wins all the money in the First Stake (if two or more players share this distinction, the one nearest the dealer's left takes preference).

Players then pick up their two face-down cards together with their face-up card and play a game of simple Brag. Winner takes the money in the Second Stake.

Money in the Third Stake is won by the player whose cards, when counted, are nearest to Thirty-one (Aces rate eleven, court cards ten each). Again, if two players hold equal cards, the player on dealer's left takes precedence.

Napoleon (or Nap)

Any number of players from two to six may play and each receives five cards, dealt singly, from a complete pack.

Beginning with the one on the dealer's left, players have the right to declare the number of tricks they think they can make. If one says 'Napoleon' (or simply, 'Nap') he indicates that he intends to make all five tricks in whist fashion (Ace high, deuce low).

If Nap is not called, then the player who made the highest declaration of tricks starts by laying a card face up before him. That card determines the trump suit. The others, in order, must follow suit whenever possible, or trump or throw away. The highest card of the lead (trump) suit takes the trick; the winner of it leads on to the next and so on until the caller has either made the number of tricks he said he would, or fails.

If he succeeds, he is paid a previously agreed stake from the others corresponding to the number of declared tricks. For example, if he declared three tricks and wins them, he receives three chips from every other player. He pays three chips to the others if he fails in his attempt.

If a caller makes more tricks than he declared,

he is only paid for those he called; similarly, if he makes no tricks, he pays for only those he called.

If a player who called Nap (all five tricks) is successful, then he receives double; but still pays single if unsuccessful.

The round over, the deal passes to the next man on the left, and continues.

Fan Tan (or 'Play or Pay')

The object of this game is to lose all the cards in your hand. A full pack is used and any number of players over three can take part.

Before the cards are dealt out, one at a time, each player puts an agreed number of chips into the kitty. Sometimes, one or more players will receive more cards than others. This does not matter (although some rules of the game say that those with fewer cards are obliged to put in an extra chip).

Ace is low and the player on dealer's left must lay a seven if he has one. If not, he pays a chip into the pool, and the next player must lay a seven, also with the same penalty if he cannot.

When, at last, a seven appears, it is placed in the centre of the table, face up. Players must then lay a card if possible, either a six or eight of the same suit as the laid seven, or another seven. The remaining sevens are placed one below the other on the table, and play continues by building up the correct suit sequences to the left and right of the master sevens (down to Aces on the left and up to Kings on the right).

Players who find they cannot go in turn pay one

chip into the kitty, and the turn passes to the left-hand neighbour.

The player who succeeds in losing all his cards first is the winner, and takes the kitty together with one chip for every card his opponents still hold.

There are some penalties: any player who passes when he could play, pays three chips into the kitty. If he passed when he held a seven, he pays five chips to the holders of the six and eight of the same suit.

Russian Bank (Crappette)

This is a game for two players, and is based on solitaire. Two packs of 52 cards are used, each pack having different backs.

Cards rank King high to Ace low.

The players draw, the lower taking choice of seat, pack and leading play. Each player lays out the cards as follows:

12 (or 13) cards are dealt face down and form the stock at dealer's right. Four cards are then dealt face up above the stock and in column extending towards the opponent. (Space allowing two further columns of cards is required between these initial columns). The tableau is formed by these eight cards. The remainder of the pack is the hand and this is placed face down to the left and below the tableau columns.

The foundations are the Aces which must be placed between the tableau columns immediately on becoming available. The order of building on the foundations is in suit and sequence.

The object of the game is to be the first to play

out the cards of hand and stock.

In turn, each plays as far as he can, a turn ending when a card cannot be played from the hand, or when an opponent calls 'stop' due to an error in play.

Cards available for play are those from tableau, hand or stock. To place a card on a tableau pile, it must be of opposite colour and immediately next lowest in rank; for example, Three Hearts on Four Clubs or Six Spades on Seven Diamonds. A tableau space may be filled from stock or hand. A player may place a matching card on his opponent's waste pile or stock, but the card must match in suit and be immediately below or above in sequence; for example, Five or Seven of Diamonds on Six of Diamonds.

Playing Order: a player may not turn up the top stock card until all cards possible have been built on the foundations within the first turn. After this, the uppermost stock card may be up-faced, and when it is played, the next is up-turned and so on.

Stock cards must be placed on the foundations in preference to tableau if there is possible choice.

A stock card which can be played in tableau prohibits hand cards being up-turned until the stock card is played.

A turn consists of turning up the hand cards one by one and when not playable, placing the card on the waste pile, which ends the turn. Having placed the card on the waste pile, no additional moves from stock or within tableau may be made.

As the hand is exhausted so the waste pile is

turned face down and becomes the hand.

An erroneous move of a card entitles the opponent to call 'Stop', whereon the fault is shown and the card replaced. The opponent may then take the turn.

Scoring: the first player to play out his hand and stock is the winner. For each card in the opponent's waste pile and hand, one point is scored. For each card in opponent's stock, two points are scored plus 30 points bonus for game.

Hearts

This game is similar to Whist, being played by four players with a pack of 52 cards. The difference, however, is that players are not partnered, there are no trumps and taking a trick containing a heart is avoided.

Each player is dealt 13 cards in the usual manner. The cards are played as in Whist, the suit led being followed. If this is not possible, the opportunity is taken to throw away any heart held, or a high card of another suit which might later take a trick containing hearts. The winner of the trick leads the following round. When the cards are played out, the hearts in each trick won are counted, and the player holding the least wins from each of the other players a previously agreed stake for each heart held. If counters are used, play continues until one player loses all his counters, or one player wins a pre-set amount. Another method is for each player to put one counter into a 'kitty' each time a heart is taken, and this is won by a player not having taken any hearts. If each has taken a heart, or one player all the hearts, the kitty remains to be won by the next player who has not taken any hearts (providing each other player has taken at least one).

Rummy

This is one of the most popular and best known card games. Two to six players take part and each plays for himself. A pack of 52 cards including a joker is used. The cards rank as Ace high to deuce low or King high to Ace low. Deal is determined by draw or cut, the lowest card taking the deal. The dealer gives one card at a time in turn to each player until each has seven in all. The remaining cards are placed face down in the centre of the table. The top card is now turned face up and placed by the pack.

The game: the object is for each player to collect in his hand sets of three or four of a kind, i.e. treys, Kings, eights, etc., and also sequences of three or more which must be of the same suit.

In sequence Ace may count low only. From the left of the dealer in clockwise direction each player in turn must draw one card from the pack or dis-card pile, adding it to his hand and discarding another from his hand. If drawn from the pack, this card may be discarded without having to be added to one's hand. Any matched set may be placed face up on the table. In turn a player may add one or more matching cards to a set from his own hand. When in this manner a player plays out all his cards, he wins the game. If the game is still in progress and the pack has been completely drawn, the following player may take the upper-most card from the discard pile or turn the whole pile face downwards and so form a new pack and draw the top card.

Rummy: this is when a player plays out all his cards in one turn without having previously placed down any set of cards or added to any other players sets.

Scoring: the winner is paid the pip value of cards held by each individual loser irrespective of whether or not they form sets. For 'rummy' the amount is double.

A variation of this game in England differs in the following ways: sets and sequences are not declared during play: there is no matching or adding to them from any other player's hand: a hand is declared when complete and any player holding a set(s) or sequence(s) excludes them when totalling the score. In some instances it is agreed that the joker be included, which is allowed to take any value the possessor chooses.

Gin Rummy

This game is one of the many varieties of Rummy. Two or more players may play, four or above playing as partners. There are many varieties of Gin Rummy, and various methods of play according to the number taking part. Described here, however, is the basic game for two players.

A 52-card pack is used. Cards rank King high to Ace low. Each court card scores 10 points: Ace 1, and the remainder their pip value. The pack is shuffled and players draw or cut for choice of seats and deal. Cards are dealt in the usual manner, each player having ten cards each. The remainder are placed as in Rummy and as in that game the object is to form sets and/or sequences. The cards are played as in Rummy, the hand ending when a player 'knocks'. Either player may knock at any time he wishes providing any unmatched card(s) do not exceed a score of ten points. The player having knocked exposes his hand. The opponent then does the same and may add matching cards to the knocker's hand. The unmatched cards are then totalled and compared. When counting in Gin Rummy, any set in the hand of the player not having knocked, is excluded.

Scoring: the knocker wins the hand if his score is less than his opponent's and the difference in the two is to the knocker's credit.

Undercut: this is when the opponent's score is equal to, or less than the knocker's. The opponent wins the hand and scores twenty-five points, plus any difference between the totals.

Gin: this is when a knocker does not hold any unmatched card in his hand. In this event, the opponent may not match any cards in the knocker's hand from that of his own. The score won by the knocker is 25 points plus any difference in totals.

The score is recorded as follows: should 'A' win the first hand by four points, that amount is written down; should he next win by seven points, this is added to the previous score.

The game is won by the first player to reach one hundred points, to which is added a further hundred bonus points for game. Should the opponent not have won any hand during that game the winner scores an outright victory. Otherwise, each player scores twenty-five points for every hand won. The two total scores are then compared, the higher score winning.

Cribbage

It is thought that cribbage was invented by Sir John Scuchling in the earlier half of the 17th century. At this time there was in existence a game called 'Noddy', and cribbage is supposed to have derived from 'Noddy'.

Two to four players may play, and the most popular game is four people playing as two teams. The variations of the game are two, three and four handed cribbage for five, six or seven card hands. A full pack of cards is used and scores noted on a cribbage board which consists of a wooden frame drilled with holes. There are four rows of thirty holes in each, which are subdivided into blocks of ten. In addition there are two game holes, drilled at each end of the board which serve to hold the pegs at the start of game. Each player has two pegs with which to mark his score. The first peg marks the total score and the rear peg is brought forward with each score, being advanced the appropriate number of holes beyond the first peg. The peg travels 'up' the outer row of holes and 'down' the inner ones.

The Ace is the lowest card and King ranks highest. In counting, the Kings, Queens, and Jacks equal ten, and the remaining cards equal their own value, Ace being the value of one. The object of the game is to score a set number of points which is sixty-one points, if five cards are dealt, or one hundred and twenty-one if six cards are dealt. In a two or three handed game each player scores individually.

Four Handed Cribbage

At the start of each game, players cut for deal and the lowest takes the deal. Dealing is clockwise and, also in this order, each player in turn deals five cards. The remainder are placed face down in the centre of the table. Each player then views his cards and selects one for the 'throw out', the card being placed face downwards on the table. This lead is taken by the player to the left of the dealer and then each player follows in clockwise direction. The cards thrown out now form the 'crib' and are placed face downwards by the side of the dealer where they remain until the end of that hand. The player to the right of the dealer now cuts the pack and the dealer withdraws the lowermost card of the pack and places it face upwards on top of the pack. This is the 'turn-up' or 'starter' and should it be Jack of any suit the dealer claims 'two for his heels' (2 points), but the claim must be made before the first card of the hand is played.

The cards are now played, the player to the left of the dealer leading. Each in turn place a card face upwards on the table until all have been exposed. As cards are placed, their numerical value is called out by the player and each card played is totalled to the previous amount until '31' in all is reached. On reaching '31', the cards played are turned face downwards on the table and counting starts again, the last player commencing. A player must 'pass' if by playing a card he would exceed the count of 31. During play, the following score: (a) 15's – when a card is played bringing the total call to fifteen, the player gains two points. (b) Pairs – a card played, having the same value as that placed by the previous player scores two points for the last player. (c) 'Pair Royal' – the playing of a card the same value as the two cards previously played—six points. (d) 'Double Pair Royal' – is the addition of a fourth card of the same value as the previously played three cards and scores twelve (although court cards have the value of ten, in pairing they must appear Jack for Jack, King for King, etc.). (e) 'Sequences' or 'Runs' – A player placing a card which forms an unbroken numerical sequence of three or more cards gains as many points as cards in the sequence, for example 3, 4, 5, or 5, 3, 4, would score three points for the last card player; 3, 4, 3, 5, however, would not score for the appearance of the second three breaks the true run. The court cards may also preclude runs but Ace cannot be included as it holds the lowest card value. (f) 'The Go' – the player placing the card which brings the total to thirty-one scores two points. (g) Compound Scores – these are a combination of any of the above, that is, sequences with fifteens or thirty-one and pairs with fifteens and thirty-one.

After the cards have been played, each player

takes up his own cards and shows them. The first
player to do so is the one to the left of the dealer.
All players score their hands in rotation and scores
gained in the beginning are as follows: the starter
may be used to assess the score in each hand and
the crib. In scoring, any card in the hand may be
used more than once providing it combines with
different cards to produce the score; for example,
a hand with a run of 2, 3, 4 scores in itself. If the
starter should be either a 2, 3 or 4 then it can be
combined to make a second score for the hand.
(1) Any combination of cards totalling fifteen –
two points. (2) A pair of cards of the same value –
two points. (3) Pair Royal – six points and over-
rides any score for pairs. (4) Double Pair Royal –
twelve points and cancels out scoring on pair and/or
Pair Royal. (5) Flush: four cards in a hand of one
suit – four points: if also the same suit as the turn
up, five points are scored. (6) 'One for his Nob' – if a
player holds the Jack of the same suit as the turn
up, he claims one point.

Eight Points – Double run in a run of three with
one card duplicated e.g. 3, 4, 5, 5.

Ten points – Double run in a run of four with one
card duplicated, e.g. 3, 3, 4, 5, 6.

Fifteen Points – Triple run in a run of three with
one card triplicated e.g. 3, 3, 3, 4, 5.

Sixteen points – A run of three with two different cards duplicated e.g. 3, 3, 4, 5, 5.

The dealer is the last to assess the score of his
hand to which he also adds that of the crib. When
scoring the crib, a flush cannot be claimed unless
of the same suit as the turn-up.

Penalties: (1) A dealer must re-deal if a wrong number of cards are dealt; if not dealt one at a time; if the pack is incomplete; if in dealing a card is exposed or if a card is 'faced' in the pack. (2) If after forming the crib a hand is found to have the wrong number of cards, a new deal may be demanded or the opponent(s) may score two and rectify the misdeal without a re-deal. If the crib is found to be incorrect but all hands correct, then the opponents of the dealer score two and the crib is rectified without a deal. Should more than one hand or crib be incorrect there must be a new deal, and players who held a correct hand score two. (3) Any player not playing when able to is not allowed to rectify the error after the next card is played. Cards withheld erroneously are considered dead and may not be played or scored from by the offender. The opponent may score two points. (4) 'Muggins': An overlooked score may be credited to the opponent should he call 'Muggins'. This is optional and if not included in the game no penalty is enforced. (5) An error in pegging: if insufficient this must be corrected before playing the next card, or forfeited. If in excess the correction must be made on demand before the next cut or deal, and the opponent scores two points.

Two Handed Cribbage

This is played like the four handed game with five or six cards. Each player places two cards in the crib, and the player not dealing automatically scores three points to offset this disadvantage. On calling 'go' each player plays in turn until 31 or the nearest to that amount is reached.

Three Handed Cribbage

This is like the four handed game. There may be three cards only in the crib or this may be made up to four by adding one from the pack. Each player is dealt five cards.

Seven-Card Cribbage

Seven cards are dealt, two of which are placed in the crib. Game is 181 points.

Newmarket

A fast-moving game suitable for any number above three. The Ace of spades, King of diamonds, Queen of hearts and Jack of clubs from a spare pack are laid face up on the table.

Having previously agreed upon a maximum stake (usually a multiple of four which we shall presume to be four pennies) each player places his bet on the four cards in any way he chooses. For example, all four pennies are placed on the Jack of diamonds or, alternatively, two pennies on the Jack and a penny each on the Ace of spades and King of hearts. The player might even decide to lay a penny on each of the four cards. The dealer always lays double the stake (in our example, eight pennies) also in any order.

He then deals out a full pack of cards, one by one, with an extra hand which is never used but serves to create 'stops' in sequence.

Players must lay the lowest cards in their hand (Ace is low) and the man on the dealer's left begins.

If his lowest card is the Ace of clubs, he lays it down in front of him, calling it by name. The holder of the next lowest card of the same suit—the two of clubs—plays and names it; and so on until a halt is called by the existence of the extra hand.

When a halt is made, the last player to have laid a card starts off another round by laying the lowest card of any suit he chooses.

It often happens that one player will have a run of cards which he must lay all at the same time, thus reducing his hand considerably. The whole aim of Newmarket is to become the first to lose all one's cards and, if possible, in the course of so doing to lay one of the four master cards and take all the money staked on it.

When a player succeeds in using all his cards, he receives from each of the others one chip (or any agreed amount) for each card left in their hands. When during the course of a game a player lays down a card corresponding to one of the four master cards, he receives all the money on that particular card.

Any unclaimed money is left to mount up until it is eventually won or divided among the players by an agreed method.

Calculation

One pack of cards is required from which an Ace, Deuce, Trey and Four are removed. These form the foundations and are placed in a row. The object now is to build on each foundation twelve cards irrespective of suit as follows:

A, 2, 3, 4, 5, 6, 7, 8, 9, 10, J, Q, K,
2, 4, 6, 8, 10, Q, A, 3, 5, 7, 9, J, K,
3, 6, 9, Q, 2, 5, 8, J, A, 4, 7, 10, K,
4, 8, Q, 3, 7, J, 2, 6, 10, A, 5, 9, K.

The remaining cards (forty-eight) are stock, from which cards are turned up one by one and played either on the foundations or waste pile.

Four waste piles may be formed by each foundation, the top card of which may be played on a foundation when possible; otherwise it cannot be moved.

Canfield

One pack of cards is used.

Lay-out: thirteen cards are counted off and placed face up on the left (this is stock). The next card is the first foundation and placed to the right of the stock, above it and face up. Level to the stock, four cards are placed in a row, each face up, forming the tableau.

The object of the game is to build up four foundations. Example: if the first foundation is five of hearts, then the five of each other suit is placed along it as obtained, these are then built up adding 6, 7, 8, 9, 10, J, Q, K, A, 1, 2, 3, 4, in that order and keeping to each specific suit.

From the hand, three cards at one time are up-turned, the upper being available for play and each lower card as revealed following play of the upper card(s). As these cards are up-turned, so the waste pile is formed and as all the hand becomes the waste pile, this then is over-turned and used as the hand again, replaying as described.

Building: the tableau cards are built on from the hand, stock and tableau itself. Red is placed on black and vice versa, the card being placed onto one immediately next highest in rank. Example: nine of clubs on ten of diamonds or, Queen of hearts on King of spades.

A space occurring in the tableau is filled by the uppermost stock card. The game continues thus until it is played out, i. e. all four foundations built up, or until it is not possible to play any further cards.

Klondike

One pack of 52 cards is used.

The cards are set out in seven columns, the first consisting of one up-turned card; the second, two cards of which the uppermost is face up; the third, three cards of which the uppermost is face up and so on. These are placed in rows, being dealt from left to right.

The foundations are the four Aces and these are placed above the tableau as they become available. These are built up in suit from Ace to King, which is the object of the game.

The building is as in Canfield, i.e. red and black and vice versa being placed on a card immediately next in rank and obtained from stock, tableau or waste pile. As the turned card on each column becomes moved in play, then the next upper card of the column is up-faced.

Any space occurring in the tableau may only be filled by Kings. After dealing the tableau, the rest of the pack becomes stock. This may be played in threes as in Canfield. Alternatively, the stock cards are up-turned one by one, in which case it may be only played through once. The waste pile is formed from stock cards which cannot be played, though its uppermost card may be included in play whenever possible.

'I Doubt It'

This game is particularly suitable for mixed players and provides much fun especially when as many as ten players are involved at the same time. Any number to thirteen may play.

One pack of 52 cards is used by five or fewer players. When six or more play, two packs of 52 cards are required, which are then shuffled together. The object of the game is to play out all one's cards.

Cards rank Ace high to deuce low.

The cards are dealt round as far as they will go in the order of threes, until the last round when they are dealt singly.

Playing the cards: the first player (to the left of the dealer) places one, two, three or four cards face down on the table and states a rank. Example: the player calls 'two Aces', placing down two cards. The actual cards placed may not be Aces, which means the player's statement need not be truthful. Anyone of the players is now allowed to dispute the statement by saying 'I doubt it'. The 'doubted' cards are then exposed and if the doubter's assumption is correct, the player of the cards must take them up together with all other cards on the table and place them in his own hand. If the player's statement was correct, then the doubter must take all the cards on the table into his hand.

If there is no doubt the cards remain as played. The game continues with each successive player placing down one to four cards and calling the rank immediately below the last one called, i.e. first player calls Aces; second Kings; third Queens and so on. Aces are called after deuces. Thus, each player can place down whatever cards of that specific group are held in his hand. The game ends and is won when the player plays out his last card.

A player is allowed to state that specific cards are not held, when in fact they may be, i.e. to say 'I have no fours', though one may be held.

Three-Card 'I doubt it'

This is another form of the above game. The cards are dealt evenly, i.e. an equal number to each player, and those remaining are placed face down in the centre of the table. In turn each player places three cards face down on the table and states the rank immediately next above the one stated by the preceding player. The first player, however, may choose whatever rank he desires. Thus, the first player may call 'three fives', the second must say 'three sixes', the third 'three sevens' and so on. As a player holds only one or two cards he draws from the remainder of the pack, so that he has three cards to place down on the table. When a player successfully plays out his last three cards, the game ends and he wins.

Double Rum

This game is a form of Rummy. It is suitable for a group of five or more players. Although it is not a game without skill, it does not demand great concentration. It is suitable for social occasions and easily followed by those unfamiliar with it. Double Rum was the first Rummy game played with two packs and is also known as Coon-Can.

Two full 52-card packs are used with two jokers, making 106 cards in all, used as one pack. Ace may rank high or low. Each player is dealt ten cards. The joker is a wild card, and can be used in any set or sequence. A joker in a sequence may be moved once when 'laying off' (i.e. adding to a sequence already formed), providing the joker is not included in the middle of a sequence. Example: if joker represents three diamonds in a sequence (joker, four diamonds, five diamonds), the three diamonds may displace the joker; but should the sequence be three diamonds, joker, five diamonds, the joker may not be displaced. The two diamonds or six diamonds may be added to the sequence.

Scoring: for each joker held in the hand, fifteen points, for each Ace, eleven points. The remaining cards score as in Rummy.

All Fours

This is a game of English origin from which various forms have been developed. The main feature is the scoring. Outlined here is the basic game (this game is termed Seven Up in the United States).

Two to four persons may play, and if four, they

play as partners, two against two. A full pack of 52 cards is used. The cards rank Ace high, deuce low. The players are dealt two sets of three cards, i.e. six in all. The remaining cards form the stock, of which the top card is up-turned. Should this be a Jack, the dealer scores one point. The object of the game is to be the first to score seven points, which constitutes game.

Scoring: four particular items contribute towards the score, hence—'All Fours'.

High: the highest trump dealt scores one point to the receiver.

Low: the lowest trump dealt scores one point to the receiver.

Jack: one point to winner of trick containing Jack trumps, or one to dealer if up-turned as trump card.

Game: one point to the player winning tricks containing scoring cards added to the highest total.

Scoring Cards: Each Ten – 10, Aces – 4, Kings – 3, Queens – 2, Jacks – 1. Playing the game: if the highest hand is not satisfied with his cards he may 'beg', in which case the dealer is required to give a point, by saying 'Take One'. Otherwise, the dealer must give three more cards to each player and turn up another card. Should this be the same suit as the previous trump card, the procedure is repeated until a different suit appears when another Jack is turned up, and this scores another point for the dealer; if in the course of making the trump the stock becomes exhausted an entirely new deal is made. When the trump has been made, any further cards dealt in this process are discarded so that each player holds six only. The cards are now played as in Whist.

In the event of a tie for game, the point is scored by the non-dealer in a two-handed game; in the three and four handed game, it is not scored. The first to reach seven points wins the game. The order of precedence in scoring is High, Low, Jack, Game.

Eights

This game is a member of the 'Stops' family. Two to eight may play, but it is most suitable for two or three, or two against two. A full pack of 52 cards is used, but for six or more players, two full packs are required shuffled together. The deal is determined by distributing the cards one to each player face up and the first to receive a spade deals first. When two play, each is dealt seven cards. When more than two, each has five cards. The remainder of the pack forms the stock, which is placed face down in the centre of the table. The top card is up-turned and placed separately, this being the starter. Should this card be an eight, it is replaced *in* the pack and the uppermost card turned up again. The object of the game is to play out one's cards, the first to do so scoring points from cards held by each other player to values as follows:

Eights equal 50, Aces, Kings, Queens, Jacks, Tens equal 10, and all the other cards their pip values.

Playing the cards: from the left of the dealer, each player in turn is required to place on the starter pile a card which matches in rank or suit.

For example: Queen of hearts on Queen of diamonds or two of diamonds on Queen of diamonds. All eights are wild cards and can be placed in turn whatever the top starter pile card may be. When playing an eight, the player must call out a suit which the next card should be, but not a denomination. The following player must place a card of the suit called, or another eight. Cards are drawn from the stock pile until one is obtained that can be played. When the stock is exhausted, a player passes his turn when unable to play. Should the player wish to draw from the stock pile, even though he is able to play, he may do so.

Should a game become blocked and no hand be played out the player with the lowest count scores the difference between his amount and that of the other players.

When four play the game in two pairs, both partners must have played out their cards before scoring takes place.

The first player or partnership to reach 500 points wins the game.

CHILDREN'S CARD GAMES

Pig

This game is for children or adults or a mixed group of both. Three to thirteen players can take part.

The number of cards used depends on the number of players. Four cards of one denomination are required per player, and if there are six players, the cards deuce to seven inclusive of each suit may be used.

The object of the game is to make a set of four cards of the same rank, and not to be the last to observe that this has been achieved by a player.

Playing the cards: the players look at their cards and then each passes one to the left and picks up the one passed from the right. This continues until one player has a set, for example, four fours, or four tens. This player then continues to hold his cards, but places a finger to his nose. As each player observes this he does the same. The last to do so is 'Pig'.

Concentration (Memory)

This is a good game for mixed players of any number from two. Even those who may never have played cards before can participate in this game.

A full pack of 52 cards is used which is dealt out one at a time face down over the entire table. No two cards should be touching. The object of the game is to take cards in pairs, i.e. two threes, two Queens or two nines, etc.

Playing the cards: each in turn faces up two cards, the first being left up-faced until the second has been turned up. As a pair are up-turned so they are taken and that player turns up two more cards. When a pair is not shown the two cards are replaced face down in their original position and the next player plays.

When all the cards have been paired, the game ends and the player with the most pairs is the winner.

Memory and the power of observation are put to the test in this game.

Pounce

This game is suitable for large groups and is of the Solitaire family.

Playing the cards: each player with his own pack plays a game of Canfield Solitaire. As an Ace appears, this is placed in the centre of the playing surface, Aces being the foundation. Any foundation may be built on by any player. Should two or more attempt to play on one foundation at the same time the first there has priority.

The game ends when a player has played out his stock, and he is the winner of the game.

GENERAL

Patience (also called Solitaire and Idiot's Delight)

As the name implies, this is a game for one player. There are various forms using one or more packs of 52 cards, but most versions proceed in much the same way. Given here is a basic outline. The tableau is formed by some or all cards being placed face up in some specific manner. Any other cards dealt initially with the tableau together form the 'lay-out'. Building may change the original lay-out. Some of the cards are blocked, whilst others can be brought into play immediately. 'Foundations' should first be released and played in their place, and if all the cards can be built on to the foundations the game is won.

Any of the pack not in the layout forms the 'stock' which supplies cards for introduction into play according to the particular version of the game. The waste pile consists of cards placed face up which cannot be placed on foundations or in the tableau.

Some games include in the lay-out a specific set of cards termed the stock and those cards not dealt initially then comprise the 'hand'.

The space is that produced in the tableau by placing cards elsewhere and in some games can be of value in the handling of the tableau.

The cards rank: King high to Ace low.

For games requiring a large playing area, special 'miniature' cards are available.

Double Solitaire

This is a game for two players who sit opposite each other, each having one pack of 52 cards. A player may play on his opponent's foundations, but not on his tableau. The player having the lowest card on the first column becomes the first to play. (If of equal value the upturned card on the second column decides). A player continues to play until he places a card on the waste pile, or until stopped by his opponent from making other play, when he is able to start a foundation with an Ace.

The game ends when a player plays out all the cards or when both become blocked. In the last case, the winner is the one with most cards played on the foundation.

Solo Whist

This is a game for three or four players (the version described here is for four) and is a gambling version of Whist.

Each player is dealt thirteen cards in groups of three, except for the last four cards in the pack, which are dealt singly. The final card is turned up to denote trumps.

Each player, starting on the dealer's left, is entitled to make a 'call' or 'declaration'. There are six 'calls' in Solo Whist, each of them having a different scope and value. They are as follows:

1. Proposal and Acceptance (commonly known as 'prop' and 'cop'), where two players in partnership endeavour to make eight or more tricks between them, against the others. Any player may propose that, with the aid of a partner, he will make eight tricks. If another player accepts, then it carries, always subject to no higher call being made. Each player has one call only, with the exception that the player on the left of the dealer, having originally passed, may 'accept' a proposal. Minimum stakes are paid for this call.

2. Solo. A player making this call proposes to make five tricks, playing against the other three players, with the trumps as shown by the turned up card. The stakes are twice the amount for prop and cop, and, as in all subsequent higher calls shown hereafter, if successful, the declarer is paid by all the three other players. If he fails in his call, he pays each of the other players. Thus, if the minimum stake is 1d, a player getting Solo would receive 2d each from each of the other three players.

3. *Misère*. There are no trumps, and the player calling misère must lose all thirteen tricks. The stakes are three times the basic amount.

4. *Abundance*. The declarer endeavours to make nine tricks, naming his own suit as trumps. He does not, however, name this suit until the bidding has ended, and no higher call has been made. In some versions of the game the originally turned up trump suit operates for the first round, and from then onwards the suit nominated by the caller. In other versions, however, the caller's trump suit operates throughout. The stake for Abundance is four times the basic amount.

The call of Royal Abundance takes precedence over Abundance, but the stakes are the same. The caller contracts to make nine tricks, with the trumps as the up-turned card.

Misère ouverte. As in Misère, there are no trumps, and the caller must lose all thirteen tricks. After the first trick has been completed, however, the caller must lay his complete hand on the table, face upwards, and thus his three opponents have the advantage of planning the play with all the caller's cards in view. The stakes are six times the basic amount.

Abondance déclarée. The highest call in Solo, the caller contracting to make all thirteen tricks. There are no trumps, and the declarer, irrespective of where he sits, makes the first lead. The hand ends, of course, should he lose a trick. The stakes are eight times the basic amount.

The stakes suggested above are not universally

played, but are the most usual. It is as well, there-fore, to agree the stakes before play begins. It is also usual to have a kitty, an agreed amount being paid by each player before play starts, to the kitty. Every time a hand is passed out, the same stakes are again added to the kitty. In some circles, the kitty is taken by the player successfully making abundance, or a higher call. In others, misère or higher takes the kitty.

Every round at Solo is complete in itself and is played to attain one of the six calls shown above. Honours are not counted, and court cards in trumps are useful only for the tricks they make.

Pontoon, 21 or vingt-et-un, also Black Jack.

This game may be played with a permanent bank, i.e. with all bets placed with the dealer re-maining in office throughout play. A second form is to have a changing bank, so that each player has a chance to be dealer. This is the most popular form for those playing the game in their homes, and is the method described here.

Two to fourteen players take part. A full pack of 52 cards is used. Card values: Ace equals 1 or 11 (as the holder desires); Kings, Queens and Jacks equal 10 and all other cards equal their face value.

The object of the game is for each player to achieve twenty-one (or as near as possible) without going beyond or exceeding twenty-one.

Who shall be first banker? This is decided by dealing the cards face up, and the first player to whom a Black Jack falls, takes the bank and is the dealer. The cards are shuffled and the top card upturned and shown to all, and then placed face up at the bottom of the pack. This serves to mark when the cards should next be shuffled.

Cards are dealt, face down, one to each player in turn including the dealer. Each player (but not the dealer) looks at his card and places a bet. (A betting minimum may be set by the players before play begins). After bets have been placed, the dealer now decides from these whether or not they indicate poor cards, (which may be so if bets are low). If the dealer wishes, he can double, which means he agrees to pay double the original stake should he lose, but then each punter must double his stake which he loses to the bank if the dealer wins.

A player may re-double if he holds a good card. For example, if a player stakes one únit and the dealer doubles, the player must then stake a further unit. If the player re-doubles, he stakes two units more, making four in all.

Another card is now dealt to each player. At this stage, if any player including the dealer has 'pontoon', it is declared. 'Pontoon' is composed of an ace and a card having the value of ten, which totals twenty-one in two cards.

If the dealer has pontoon, each player pays him double the original stake, or four times the original stake if the dealer doubled. A player who has pontoon receives the same from the dealer, and becomes dealer in the next round. If the player does not wish to be dealer, he may 'sell' the bank to any other player who wants it. Should two players have pontoon, the player nearest the dealer's left gets the bank, or they cancel each other out and the bank does not change, but they are paid out to the value of their original stakes. If no one has pontoon, the dealer takes each player in turn. The player may 'buy', in which case he is dealt a card face down, having previously added to his stake.

On the other hand, he may 'twist', on which no further bet is placed and the card is dealt face up. The dealer continues to deal cards to the player until the player 'sticks' (being satisfied with the total received), or 'busts' (exceeds twenty-one). In this case the stake goes to the dealer and the cards to the bottom of the pack. After all players have been dealt, the dealer then turns up his own cards and adds to them with face-up cards until he decides to 'stick' or 'bust'.

If the latter is the case, all players not having previously 'bust' receive their stake value from the dealer. If the dealer sticks, all those with a higher score and not 'bust' are paid their stake value by the dealer. The players who stood, but have an equal or lower count than the dealer, lose their stake to the bank.

A player who is dealt five cards without busting is immediately paid double his stake by the dealer, irrespective of the dealer's final total (this is not so in reverse for the dealer receives double for his five-card trick).

Pontoon is a game of chance rather than skill, but can be most exciting. When placing bets it is advisable to lay low stakes on low cards, and higher stakes on an Ace or a card of the value of ten. On reaching 17, the risk of 'busting' is greater.

It is usual to include in the rules a minimum count at which a player may 'stick', which is usually sixteen.

Chemin de Fer (shimmy or chemmy)

This game is a form of Baccarat which is a popular casino game. Two to thirty can take part. Five full 52-card packs are used. These are shuffled together and placed in a shoe (a dealing box delivering one card at a time) face down. Usually a croupier is present who does not actually participate in the game but advises the players on betting, the correct procedure and appropriate plays.

The first deal may be put to auction and the player offering the highest amount per stake becomes first dealer.

Amount of bank: this is the maximum stake the dealer will place and before dealing he must announce this amount. Players to the left of the dealer may in turn bet the full, or part of that amount. The dealer is not held responsible for payments on bets in excess of this.

Banco: This is a wager involving the whole bank. Any player may call this whereupon all other bets are withdrawn. Should more than one make this call, precedence goes to the player on the dealer's left. Dealing follows when all bets have been placed or when the dealer's entire bank is equalled by bets placed. The player who has the largest bet receives one card dealt face down. The dealer then deals one to himself, a second to the player, then a second to himself.

The object of the game is to achieve a count as near nine as possible, composed of two or three cards.

Card values: Court cards and tens equal ten or nought; Aces equal one; all other cards equal their pip value.

In totalling, tens are not counted (seven and eight equal fifteen but the ten is cancelled out). Therefore five is the count.

If dealer or player scores eight or nine with the first two cards, he shows his hand immediately. All bets are won by the dealer if he has this count.

If the player has the count, all bets are played by the dealer. Should each score the same, bets are withdrawn and placed again for the next deal. Each deal is a coup. But if this does not take place, the punter may draw a card which he receives face up. The dealer then also draws a card, but either may stand without drawing a card if they wish. The cards are then exposed, and the dealer pays all bets if his opponent is nearer nine, but receives all if he himself is nearer.

If the total is a tie, bets are stood off and withdrawn. Most chemin de fer games are governed by the following regulations about the decision to stand or draw:

If punter's points are ten or less, he must draw; five may stand or draw, and six or seven must stand.

If the punter stands, the dealer must stand on six or seven points, but must draw if he has five points or less.

If the punter draws an Ace, court card or ten, the

dealer must stand at four points, and must draw if less than four points.

If the punter draws a nine, the dealer must stand at four points; may stand or draw at three points, and must draw at less than three points.

If the punter draws eight, the dealer must stand at three points and if less than three points must draw.

If the punter draws seven or six, the dealer must stand at seven points, and if less than seven points must draw.

If the punter draws five or four, the dealer must stand at six points and if less than six points must draw.

If the punter draws a three or two, the dealer must stand at five points and if less than five points must draw.

The bank changes when the dealer loses a coup.

The turn of dealer rotates in clockwise direction from the left of the first dealer.

Baccarat

This game is the same as Chemin de Fer with the following exceptions:

(a) The bank does not change until the dealer wishes to retire or until the original total bank amount is lost.

(b) Three hands are dealt in each coup, one to the left and one to the right of the dealer, including himself.

(c) Bets may be placed on either right or left hand or a cheval may be bet. In the latter, the dealer pays if he loses to the two hands, but collects if he wins *both* hands. The dealer pays the two hands separately. This is a game of chance as is Chemin de Fer.

Each new dealer must announce the amount in the bank. Cards are not usually re-shuffled until the point is reached when only a few remain in play.

TRAVELLING GAMES

Here are a few ways of relieving the tedium of a long journey made by car. A word of warning first, however—these games are for *passengers* only. In the interests of Road Safety the driver's attention must not be distracted in any way.

For the majority of games a set number of points should be determined before play begins and the first player to reach this total is the winner.

Blind Judge

An object some distance ahead is selected, and all the players close their eyes. As each thinks the object has been reached, 'Now' is called and the eyes are opened. The player whose guess is most accurate scores 1 point.

Future Guess

At a time when the road behind and in front is free of traffic each player guesses what vehicle he thinks will be the next to appear. Identification may be by the particular make of the vehicle, for example, Sprite, Jaguar, etc., or by the type of vehicle, i.e. push-bike or bus. Each correct guess scores a point.

Colour or Car Score

Each player chooses a colour, which to maintain interest should be one that is not too familiar or too commonly seen. Two-toned colours may be selected, for example, yellow/grey or green/cream.

The task now is to keep watch for any cars of the chosen colour(s) and on spotting one to call out immediately. The first to do so correctly scores a point. Instead of colours a make of car may be chosen, for example, Ford Classic, Humber, etc.

Distance Guessing

A distant object along the road travelled is selected, for example a church steeple or tall chimney. Each player guesses how far distant it is. The true distance is checked from the mileometer as the object is passed. The player who makes the nearest guess scores one point.

Compose a Sentence

Each player makes a mental note of the letters on the first two car registration plates seen. Using the letters memorised he then attempts to compose a sentence, each letter being the first of a word and used in the order seen. Example: EWE and DLE – 'Enormous Waves Envelop Doris' Little Ears'; or LMP and GLA – 'Last May Percy Got Lost Abroad'. The first player to produce an acceptable sentence wins a point.

Guess the Car

Each player guesses the make of a car as it approaches. The first to make an accurate guess scores a point, but the guess must be made before the car actually passes.

Travel Through the Alphabet

Each player in turn looks for the letters on the licence plates of a car as it passes. The object of the game is for each player to collect letters making the alphabet in the correct order. Should a plate contain 2 required letters these are allowed to score providing they appear consecutively. For instance, if in the first round a player spots BAD, 'A' only is scored. Should, however, the letters be ABD, 'A' and 'B' both score since they are in correct alphabetical order. The first to complete the alphabet is the winner.

Score the Clock

This is played on the same principle as the Alphabet Game, but instead of letters, the *numbers* on the licence plates are spotted. Each player must collect 1–12 and in order. The first to do so is the winner.

Here again, if a plate contains two required numbers consecutively, these are allowed.

Tourist Suggestions

A game of alphabetical progression, played in the manner illustrated in the following example:
A says to B 'I am off to Australia. What should I do there?'

B – 'Approach Adelaide with admiration.'

B then turns to C and says 'I'm going to Bangor. What shall I do there?'

C replies 'Bathe and boat in the blue water.'

C to D 'I'm travelling to China. What ought I to do there?'

D replies 'Collect carved chopsticks.' Each player begins with a set number of points and each time he defaults a point is forfeited.

TRAVEL GAMES REQUIRING PENCIL AND PAPER

Spot Words

Each player in turn takes an approaching or passing car and scores a point for each word he is able to form by using the letters on that car's licence plate. Examples are EWE, MAD, EMU, etc. Should the registration letters of two successive cars enable a six letter word to be formed, five points are awarded. The game can continue at intervals throughout the journey or for a short period only.

Animal Spotting

A game for two or more players who divide into 2 teams. One team takes the nearside of the road, the other the offside. The object is to spot animals scoring the following number of points: dog, cat, sheep, cow, and horse, all equal 1 point, but should any of the animals bear black markings two points are scored. Rabbit, hare, or partridge equal three points. Any other animal scores five points.

Town and County

In addition to paper and pencil a car handbook is needed. Each player in turn writes down the registration letters of a passing car. The handbook is then consulted, and the appropriate town or county of registration is written down. The first player to record 20 different towns and/or counties is the winner.

50,000 Total

Each player in turn takes down the registration number of a passing car, adding each new figure to the previous one collected. The first to obtain the total of 50,000 is the winner.

Spotting in Town

This is similar to 'Animal Spotting', the players being divided into two teams, each taking one side of the car while it is travelling through a town. Each article spotted scores as follows: policeman equals 1 point; traffic light equals 2; cinema equals 3; child with parent equals 4; baby in pram equals 5; trees equal 6; flowers equal 7; dog with leash equals 8; horse and cart equals 9; church equals 10. The first team to score 100 points is the winner.

Motoring Navigation

Here are a few final suggestions for passing the time on a car journey.

1. Using a map, follow the route and name each town marked and each river crossed.

2. Take note of the mileage hourly, and work out your vehicle's average speed for the journey.

3. Make a route mileage chart, writing down each town reached, together with the distance and total mileage from the previous town or city.

4. Estimate at what time a certain point in the journey will be reached and/or how much distance will be covered within the next 30 minutes.

A GAME FOR A LONG TRAIN JOURNEY

Alphabet Cricket

Pencil, paper and a book or magazine are all that is required for this game of indoor cricket for two people. Make a note of the following code in which every letter of the alphabet has been given a 'cricketing' value as follows:

A	= 1 run	J	= 4 runs
B	= Bowled	K	= 1 run
C	= Caught	L	= L. B. W.
D	= 1 run	M	= 1 run
E	= 2 runs	N	= 1 run
F	= 1 run	O	= 0 runs
G	= 1 run	P	= 1 run
H	= Hit Wicket	Q	= 1 run
I	= 2 runs	R	= Run Out

S	= Stumped	W	= 1 run
T	= 1 run	X	= 6 runs
U	= 3 runs	Y	= 1 run
V	= 1 run	Z	= 4 runs

Each player decides which team he will be (his particular favourite county side or a special all-star eleven of famous players) and writes down the names of his players on a sheet of paper, in batting order. Toss a coin to decide who bats first.

The player who 'bowls' first opens the book at random and reads off the letters along the top line of a printed page. Meantime the 'batsman' converts each letter into a cricket score by means of the code, and keeps score.

Let us suppose the first batsman is Colin Cowdrey and that this is the sentence the bowler is reading: 'A pencil, paper and book...'

This will become:

1, 1, 2, 1, caught. Thus Colin Cowdrey only managed 5 runs before he was caught out. Record this score and then carry straight on with your next batsman who might be Ted Dexter: 2, leg before wicket. Well, Dexter didn't last long, did he? Continue with the scoring until the tenth wicket falls, whereupon the other side go in to 'bat'. Turn to a fresh page and start again at the first sentence.

Two innings should be played as in real cricket.

Marbles are popular with all ages

The Telcon Terribles of Crawley, Sussex in training

The ancient game of Five Stones
Hoola Hoop — a modern craze

Hopscotch—but the player's feet should be clear of the lines

Two variations of deck quoits

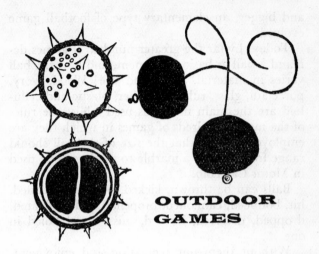

OUTDOOR GAMES

The Greeks had a word for it: 'Hepiskuros'. So did the Romans: 'Harpastum', and the Chinese: 'Tsu Chu'. Roughly translated, they all mean: 'To kick a ball made of leather with the foot'.

This ancient pastime has not lost any of its appeal, nor has it changed much. As long ago as 500 B.C. the Chinese played football as part of their military training, introducing complex technicalities of attack and defence.

But the football is by no means the oldest ball in existence. The first ball was possibly of stone or bone, crudely shaped to be rolled or thrown. Later, we do know that it was made from leather stuffed with feathers and earth. As the former was hard and solid, we may assume that the earliest kind of ball game was 'catch': then, as balls became softer and bigger, an elementary type of football game evolved.

Today, by far the greater number of games demand a ball as basic equipment, and how the ball varies in material, shape and size! Wood, ivory, porcelain, glass, rubber, leather, plastic and celluloid are the main materials used whilst the rules of the many hundreds of games in which they are employed require that the size of the ball should range from that of a marble to the huge one used in Motor Car Polo.

Balls can be thrown, kicked, punched, headed, hit, bounced, cannoned, propelled, rolled, floated, dropped, diverted, bowled, missed and holed in one.

Without them our recreation and enjoyment, and, incidentally, the size of this book, would be greatly depleted!

BALL GAMES

Circle Touch Ball

For this game a large ball is required: a beachball is ideal. In fact, although the game may be played in any open space and not only by children, it is an excellent beach game—a splendid way to warm-up after a swim!

A large circle is formed by all but one of the players. The circle players face inwards and there should be a space of approximately 5 ft. between each player. The 'odd' player stands in the centre of the circle.

The ball is now thrown from player to player

across the circle, whereupon the centre player attempts to touch the ball at any time when it is not actually held by a circle player. When he succeeds, the centre player changes places with the circle player who last threw the ball.

Mock Volley Ball

Any ball may be used, though again a beach ball is best. This game is also excellent for the beach.

Teams are formed consisting of four or five players each. In turn, each team volleys the ball into the air as many times as possible without losing control or causing it to touch the ground. The winning team is the one making the highest number of consecutive volleys.

To volley the ball, it should be directed into the air, pushed up by one or both hands; actually catching hold of the ball is not permitted.

Touch Ball

Again a large ball is required, preferably a beach ball. All but two of the players space themselves about the playing area. The ball is then passed at random between the players, but the ball must be bounced each time before a pass is made. Free movement is permitted by all the players, except by the one who is actually holding the ball who must remain on one spot.

Throughout, the two 'odd' players attempt to *touch* the ball at any time when it is not actually in the possession of another player. On making a touch, the successful 'odd' player changes places with the one who attempted the pass.

Ring the Bell

This game is more appropriate for play in the garden, where equipment may be at hand. Required: one or more beach balls, a small ring or hoop, and a bell, or any gong-like object such as an enamel mug or similar metal article.

The hoop is suspended from a branch of a tree, or in an open doorway. Suspended within the hoop is the bell, or its substitute. A line is marked, approximately 14 ft. distant from the hoop.

Each player in turn stands behind the line and attempts to throw a ball at the object within the hoop, aiming to 'ring the bell'. Scoring: 5 points are gained by 'ringing the bell'. However, should the ball pass through the hoop without 'ringing the bell', only three points are allowed. Each ball that hits the hoop only, scores one point. This game may be adapted also for team-play.

Bucket Ball Chase

One end of the playing area is marked off as a 'home' space, and in the centre of the opposite boundary a bucket is placed. One player is required to stand approximately 3 yards from the bucket, and facing it, i.e. with his back to the boundary of the 'home' space. He tries to toss the ball into the bucket.

On either side of this player, at a distance no closer than two yards, stand the remaining players. If the ball goes into the bucket, all players except the thrower swiftly dash to the safety of the 'home' area. The ball-thrower chases after the others and attempts to catch hold of a player before he can reach the 'home' boundary; the one caught then becomes the 'ball thrower' and the game re-starts.

A 'chase' cannot be made unless and until the ball remains in the bucket. Should it bounce out, another throw must be made. This game can be played on the beach with a sand-castle bucket and a ball of appropriate size.

North, South, East and West

This game may be played by any number of players on a lawn or any firm ground. A ball and a chair or four-legged stool or small table are required. The chair is placed in the centre of the playing area. The four spaces between the legs of the chair represent North, South, East and West.

At a distance of approximately 4 yards from the centre a line is marked on each of the four sides. In turn, each player now rolls the ball, aiming to pass it clearly through the two legs forming each side. Should he fail with any throw, the ball is passed to the next player in turn to throw.

Scoring: A ball through the legs representing the North side counts one point, through the East scores two points, the South three points, and the West four points.

Each player must commence at the North side and, following each successful throw, move in a clockwise direction; thus, two consecutive successes produce three points, three successes six points. A faultless round scores ten points.

After one or more rounds, the winner is the player with the highest score. Alternatively, it may be decided that the winner will be the first player to reach an agreed number of points.

Sack Ball (1)

This is a rollicking game providing plenty of excitement for children or adults. In addition to a football, a sack for each person taking part is required. Also needed are goals at each end of the playing area. For these a line is marked on the ground, and sticks or stumps form the goalposts. Each player gets into a sack, as if for a sack race, and teams are formed of equal numbers. The object of the game is for each team to score as many goals as possible by getting the ball over the opponents' goal-line. This they do as best they can, either by kicking or heading the ball. Handling is not allowed. There are no boundaries, except natural hazards. Throughout the game, each player must remain within his sack, and the general principles of Association Football laws apply.

Sack Ball (2)

This is a somewhat rougher version of the children's game previously described. Mark out a playing area of suitable size. At each end, stick two poles into the ground, 6 ft. high and 6 ft. apart. Join the tops with rope.

Any even numbers of players may take part, divided into two teams, and each must wear a sack (as for a sack race). A standard soccer or rugger ball is needed. There are no rules and the only infringements are:

(a) Getting out of one's sack.
(b) Holding on to the ball once you have been tackled by an opponent.

A point is lost for each of these offences. The object is for each team to try (a) to kick the ball through the goal-posts (thus scoring a goal) or (b) score a try in rugger fashion by touching the ball down over any part (including inside the goals) of the opponents' base-line. One point is scored for either and, at the end of an agreed period of time, the team with the most points wins.

Players will want to clutch at their sacks with their hands (although they may let them flop around their ankles provided they never step out of it), so this soccer-rugger game provides plenty of laughs as well as excitement.

Tyre Ball

A football is required, and two motor tyres which serve as goals are placed flat on the ground, one at each end of the playing area. The players form two teams of equal number and position themselves roughly as in football. The object of the game is for each side to obtain as many goals as possible, and a goal is scored only when the ball touches the ground within the tyre of the opposing side.

The referee starts the game by tossing up the ball at the centre of the playing area, and the game is re-started each time in the same way. In this game *kicking* the ball is not allowed. It must be bounced or thrown, or it may be headed. A free throw may be awarded for the following faults:

(1) Kicking. (2) Impeding a player deliberately.
(3) Tackling a player who is not holding the ball.
(4) Moving more than two steps whilst holding the
ball.

Human Target Ball

Three parallel lines are marked at a distance of
approximately 10 yards apart, but the distance
should by increased or decreased according to the
ages of those taking part.

The players are divided so that for every four
players, one player stands on the centre line; these
players are the 'human targets', who must stand
still.

The remaining players are then positioned on
the outer lines, an equal number on each, and a
ball is given to each one of these players. Those
with the balls are 'throwers' and the players on the
opposite line are 'retrievers' who return the balls.

The game begins by the 'throwers' aiming the
balls at the players on the centre line. On being
struck by a ball, a centre line player must change
places with the successful 'thrower'. No outer line
player may throw unless standing on his line.

After the game has begun, there is no fixed order
of throwing; a brisk bombardment should take
place, the retrievers picking up and returning the
balls as swiftly as possible. At set intervals, throwers
and retrievers change places.

Mock Handball

This game is suitable for a large group of players
and provides fun and good exercise. A football or

beach ball is most suitable. Also required are two receptacles for goals: buckets, tin drums, or boxes may be used. The goals are situated at each end of the playing area.

The players divide into two teams and are positioned as in Association Football.

The object of the game is for each team to get the ball into the goal of the opposing side. A goal is scored when the ball enters and remains within the receptacle which serves as a goal. The ball must be thrown or carried. It may also be rolled, but kicking is not allowed. Should a small ball be used the 'field of play' can be larger, since a small ball can be thrown further.

Three-legged Football

This is a game for a large number of players, conducted as a straightforward game of football would be, except that the players do not proceed individually but in pairs. Their inside legs are tied together with a scarf, or handkerchief, as for a three-legged race. A fairly small 'field' of play is advisable, and periods of play should be short because this game can prove exhausting.

Court Football

This is suitable for a small group from 6 to 12 in number. The playing arena, which should be of a size appropriate to the ages of the children, should have a dividing line across the centre, making two equal sections with a goal-line at either end. Players divide into two teams. Each must remain within its own half of the court, but a player may take up any position in his own half.

The game begins with the ball being thrown up between the two team leaders in the centre of the court. Then each attempts to 'tip' it with the hands to one of his own team players.

The object is for each team to try and score goals by kicking the ball over the goal-line at the base of the opponents' court. There is no specific goalkeeper, and each player must both defend and attack.

To score a goal the ball must be kicked. After each goal the game is re-started by the referee throwing the ball up at the centre, the only time during the game when handling is allowed. A player entering his opponents' half of the court is penalised by the award of a free kick to his opponents.

This may also be played as Court Hockey, with walking sticks used to propel a tennis ball.

Cap Ball

This is a schoolboy game often seen in the playground. Each boy places his cap in line by a wall, and stands 5 ft. away from his own cap. A ball is then rolled by one boy, who attempts to get the ball into a cap. When he achieves this, the owner of the particular cap in which the ball landed must retrieve the ball.

Meanwhile, the remaining players scatter swiftly. The player with the ball must now throw at an escaping player and attempt to hit him with it. If his throw is not successful a stone is placed in his cap. If he does hit the escaping player then a stone is put into the cap of the one hit.

Whichever of the two players receives the stone in his cap re-starts the game. As soon as a player gets three stones in his cap, he is eliminated from the game.

Tail Ball

This is a game for a group of players not exceeding sixteen in number. The players divide into two equal teams. One team forms a large circle facing inwards, while the other forms a straight line, one behind the other, within the circle.

The circle players have a soft ball, with which they attempt to hit the tail-end player of the other team. The leader of this team, however, has the responsibility of avoiding the 'tail' being hit by dodging from side to side, with his team following behind him. The leader *only* may ward off the ball with his hands; the hands of each remaining team member should be around the waist of the player in front of him and the whole line should remain unbroken.

Each time the last player is hit, he goes to the head of the team and the game continues thus until all have been hit, when the teams change places and the game re-starts.

Scrummage

This is a short, exciting game in which the players divide into threes, one set of three opposing the other set. Each stands facing the other. A ball is tossed up high in the air between the two sets and the team to catch it scores one point. Each player is allowed to try and prevent his opponents from securing the ball and capture it himself, and an exciting struggle may take place. The throw is taken by each team in turn and ten points make a game.

Tower Ball

This game may be played almost anywhere, and the simple equipment required will readily be at hand amongst campers. A loose tripod is assembled from brooms, sticks, or tent poles, and tied together at the top. The top ends should be able to support a large ball.

Players are divided so that for every four players who are 'attackers', there is one 'guard'. The 'guards' remain within a large circle drawn round the tripod, and the attackers are outside the circle. The 'attackers' have one ball or more, preferably footballs or beach balls, with which they attempt to dislodge the ball balanced on the tripod.

An 'attacker' who achieves this changes places with the nearest 'guard'. It is permissible to hit the tripod in order to displace the ball. Kicking the ball, however, is not allowed. Should a 'guard' dislodge the ball while defending, he is required to change places with the nearest 'attacker'.

Bicycle Football

A large safety area is required for this game since each player (except the goalkeeper) is mounted on a bicycle. This is definitely not a game to be played in the street. The principles of ordinary football are followed as closely as possible. The ball may be moved by the front wheel as well as kicked, but handling is not allowed, except by goalkeepers.

Bottle Ball

Any number of players may take part in this game, which can be played in any large open space. A football or beach ball is required, and two strong bottles or stone jars for goals, which are placed one at each end of the field. The players divide into equal teams.

Each team aims to knock over its opponents' bottle and so score a goal. The ball may be thrown *only*—kicking is not allowed, nor may any player carry the ball.

If desired, the bottles can be placed in circles approximately 6 ft. in circumference, the circle being forbidden territory, within which no player is allowed to penetrate.

Glide Ball

A game for swimmers only, played waist deep in water. This is particularly suitable for camping holidays if there is a stream nearby. The simple equipment required is a length of rope, which is stretched across the stream approximately 6 ft. above the water surface, and a ring threaded on the rope, to which is attached a length of cord. Suspended on the cord is a football or beach ball. The ball should be close to the surface of the water.

Two teams of five players each take part, each team having a 'goalie' standing on opposite banks of the stream. The remaining four players of each team stand on the banks facing each other. The ball is in midstream. At the signal to start each team jumps into the stream and swimming, walking or running, attempts to get the ball back into the grasp of its own 'goalie'. When this has been achieved, one point is scored. The ball is centred after each goal.

Catch and Keep the Ball

This game may be played in a wooded glade by campers, ramblers or picnickers. Select a tree branch, 8 or 9 ft. above the ground and extending well clear of the tree. With a length of string, suspend a football from this branch so that the ball is only 2 ft. from the ground.

Players form a circle round the ball and number off. The even numbers constitute one team, the odds another. One side is allowed the ball and it must try to keep it from its opponents. The opposing team attempts to seize the ball and when it succeeds, keeps it, and the game begins again.

Should there be only a few players, a tennis ball may be used. The leader throws the ball and any player attempts to catch it; whoever does so makes the next throw. One point is awarded for each catch. The players must keep their places in the circle in both forms of the game.

Tree Ball

This game may be played in the garden, in a wooded copse, or wherever a suitable tree is available. Select a tree situated in a clear level area. Around the tree trunk near ground level, knot a strong length of cord securely so that it cannot slip.

The cord should be 20 to 30 ft., to the end of which is fastened a football. Two or four players may take part at a time, and compete as individuals or pairs, each remaining within their own space around the tree. The ball is now kicked by either side, but in opposite directions, one side kicking the ball clockwise, the other anti-clockwise. Each kicks whenever there is an opportunity to do so.

Eventually, as the cord winds round the trunk, the ball will come to rest by the tree. If the ball touches the tree, or if any player becomes entangled in the cord, a free kick is awarded to the non-offenders.

Pick-a-Back Polo

A game for two teams, each consisting of four to ten players. The players pair off, each couple armed with a walking stick, umbrella or golf stick. One tennis ball is required, and a goal should be marked at each end of the playing area.

At the signal to start, one player mounts the back of his partner and each 'horse-and-jockey' team aims to score by driving the ball into the opposing goal with the aid of the stick.

Jostling and bumping is part of the game, but holds are not allowed, neither may players hit the ball while dismounted. Pairs may change places whenever they wish.

Patball

This is a game for two players at a time. They stand face to face, a small circle having been marked on the ground between them. Players then proceed in turn to pat the ball into the circle. A point is lost each time a player steps into the circle, misses the ball, or puts it out of the circle. Fifteen points constitute one game.

Rounders

Rounders can be played as a serious team sport, or purely for fun. In Britain it is a well organised sport, involving specific rules and a specially marked playing pitch, diamond-shaped, with four posts or bases. The version given here is an informal one, suitable for a small field or garden, where the distance between the bases may vary according to the space available. This is often called Danish Rounders. It is easily adaptable to any even number of players, who are divided into two equal teams. Eight a side is ideal.

According to the size of your garden or playing area, map out your pitch. Space the four bases as far apart as the age and skill of the players allows. The bases can be marked by chairs, posts, or baskets, and are called, in turn, first base, second base, third base and fourth or home base. (See fig. 11.) Near to the first base is the service circle and, just a few yards away from that, the batting line.

The teams toss to decide who will bat and who will field. One member of the fielding team acts as server and his team-mates spread themselves about the pitch in strategic positions, at least one standing at each base, and one acting as backstop behind the batter.

The batting sides line up, one behind the other

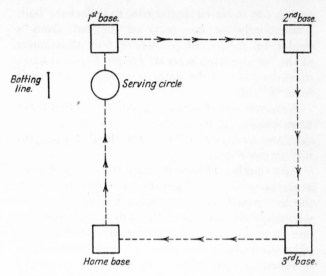

Rounders (Fig. 11)

on the batting line. The first takes up his position, using as his 'bat' either a clenched fist or stout stick. The server throws the ball (a tennis ball is best) directly at him. The server must employ no tricks when throwing, but make simply a slowish under-arm or over-arm delivery, giving the batsman plenty of chance to hit the ball really hard.

Whether he hits or misses the ball, the batsman *must* always run for the first base as fast as he can. The batsman aims to hit the ball as far away as possible so that he has time to run right through first, second and third bases and return to home base before any fielder can return the ball to the server standing in the circle. The server is allowed to run out of his circle in order to collect the ball. Immediately he has received the ball from a fielder he shouts 'Stop!' whereupon all runners of the batting team who are caught between bases must drop out of the game until it is their team's turn to field.

A runner who has reached one of the first three bases before the server shouts 'Stop' is considered safe, and he may rest there until the next opportunity to move on.

Any number of runners may stand at one base at the same time, and anyone who can safely reach the home base scores a run for his side. A player who succeeds in running through all four bases at one go scores two runs, and can also call back one of his team-mates (already 'out') to resume batting.

When the ball is caught by a fielder straight from the strike, the batter is out and so are all those not safely at a base at the time. A whole side is out when it no longer has a player in reserve to take over the batting. The two teams then change sides.

Korfball

This again can be played as a serious team sport or quite informally using home-made equipment. The game of Korfball was invented by the Dutch and enjoys considerable popularity in Europe. It is a variation of handball and basketball, essentially for the outdoors. Teams consist of six men and six women who play on a field 100 yards by 45 yards.

When playing purely for fun, however, the court

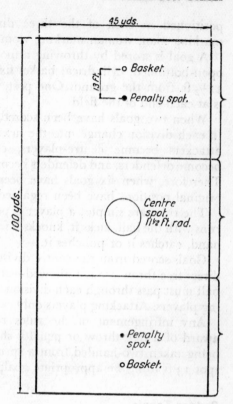

Korfball (Fig. 12)

can be of any convenient size, and the equipment can be home-made, but twelve a side is the most convenient number. (See fig. 12.)

Two men and two women from each team are

251

positioned in each of the three divisions, man marking man, woman marking woman.

A goal is scored by throwing a football into an open-bottomed, cylindrical basket fixed to a post 11 ½ ft. from the ground. One post, with basket, is at each end of the field.

When two goals have been scored, the players in each division change into the next, so that the attackers become centre-players, centre-players become defenders, and defenders become attackers. Therefore, when six goals have been scored, the original positions have been regained.

The rules are simple: a player is penalised if he runs with the ball, kicks it, knocks it from another's hand, catches it or punches it.

Goals scored from the centre division or from a direct free throw are not allowed—at all times the ball must pass through each division to the attacking players. Attacking players only can score goals.

Any infringement of the rules results in the award of a free throw or penalty shot, the latter being taken two-handed from a specially marked spot 13 ft from the appropriate goalpost.

Padder Tennis

This is Lawn Tennis in miniature, played on a court 39 ft. long by 8 ft. wide (half the size of an official Lawn Tennis court) using special 'padders', which are bats made from 5-ply wood. They have a thick handle 5 in. long and their overall length is 16 in. The face of the bat is 8½ in. wide.

Sponge rubber balls are used and the net is 2 ft. 3 in. high.

The game is played in exactly the same manner as lawn tennis, using over-head services into the court diagonally opposite, with rallies, faults and identical scoring. However, many people prefer to make up their own rules, and it would be quite in order to play as you would in Quoit Tennis (details of which are given on page 309).

In this case, the object would be to score 15 points for 'game', serving the ball under-arm with your padder.

Doubles also can be played, under Quoit Tennis or Lawn Tennis rules.

Spade Ball (or Stick Ball)

This is a team game for five or more players per side. A beach ball is required, together with two sticks or, if played on the beach, two sand spades.

Mark out a court approximately 30 ft. wide by 60 ft. long, and mark out a centre line. Eight feet in from each base line, draw a circle with a radius of 6 to 8 ft. and push the stick or spade in the centre of each circle.

The object of the game is to score points by knocking down or hitting your opponents' sticks with your ball.

Briefly the rules are:

(1) The start and re-start is in the centre of the court between two opposing players, and the ball is thrown up by the referee.

(2) No running is allowed when in possession of the ball.

(3) No kicking—and hand passes only are allowed.

(4) The goal-keeper (or stick guard) may not leave his circle, neither can any other player enter it.

(5) If a goal-keeper accidentally knocks down his own stick, this loses a point for his team.

(6) Two points are awarded for each successful goal.

Overhead-ball Rounders

A simple Rounders court is marked out with a base line and three bases approximately twelve yards apart. The game is for two equal teams and is scored as in Rounders (i.e. a run through the bases from base-line to base-line). Having decided who will bat and who will field, the batsmen line up behind the base-line, each in turn moving up to strike the ball (a beach ball, or slightly smaller soft ball would be most suitable).

The fielding team take up strategic positions and elect one member to serve or pitch the ball. He throws it to the batsman between shoulder and waist level.

Using his hand, the batsman must hit the ball as far away as possible and then run round the court to each base in turn and back to the base-line again. As soon as a fielder retrieves the ball, he throws it to the server, whereupon all the fielders run to form a line behind the server. The ball is then passed backwards, over the heads, from the server down to the last man.

The batsman is out if he has not returned to the base-line before the last of the fielders receives the ball from his team-mate immediately in front of him. A batter is also out if the ball he hit is caught by a fielder.

When all a team's batsmen are out, the sides change roles.

Garden Bowls

There are many variations of the official game of Bowls played outdoors. If the lawn is even and long enough, and if the grass is short and smooth, so much the better. In full-scale Bowls, each player propels a wooden bowl towards a smaller white porcelain ball (known as the 'jack') aiming to make it stop nearer to the 'jack' than the bowl of his opponents.

Here we are only concerned with an informal garden version. The most popular way of playing is with tennis balls and a stick or peg. You can play singles (one player against another, each rolling four balls); pairs (two against two, each playing individually in turn), and teams (four players to team, each rolling one ball in turn).

Having driven your peg or stick into one end of the lawn, your aim is to roll your ball towards it so that it comes to rest against it, or closer to it than that of any of your opponents. It makes things easier if one team uses tennis balls which have been clearly marked.

Balls which lie in better positions than the best

ball of your opponents are the only ones to count. And, as you are permitted to try to knock away the best balls of your opponents, the last throw could score highest of all.

Award three points for the ball which rests nearest to the peg; two points for the next nearest ball; one point for the third nearest. First to reach 21 points (or any other previously agreed score) wins.

Philadelphia Kick Ball

Another variation of Rounders, this time of American origin, which explains its name. The court is marked out as shown (See fig. 13). A beach ball or smaller soft ball is ideal.

Two equal teams are formed, one kicking and the other fielding (this is decided by the toss of a coin). The ball is placed in home base, then kicked into the field of play as far forward as possible by the first kicker. He then runs through each base and back home. This counts as one home run if completed before the base guard has had the ball returned to him and is able to bounce it in the home base.

A kicker may remain at any of the bases should he not be able to complete a home run but no more than two players may be at the same base at the same time.

If the ball is bounced in the home base by the base guard while any kicking players are between bases, these are out. The side scoring the highest number of home runs are the winners. A player

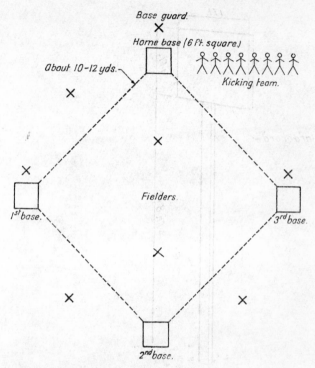

Philadelphia kick-ball (Fig. 13)

who has stopped at a base does not score a run, though he may kick again if the circuit is subsequently completed.

Stoolball

Stoolball is like Cricket in that a batsman has to defend his wicket with a bat. He can score runs, including boundaries, and be bowled, caught or

257

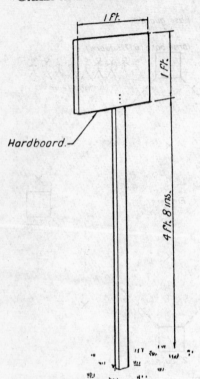

Stoolball (Fig. 14)

run out. There are byes, wides and overs; and fielders include a wicket-keeper.

Historians tell us that modern Cricket is a derivative of Stoolball, but the latter game is still widely played for its own sake, mostly by women, and it has its own governing association. For our purposes, we shall describe an adaptation of this ancient game which is suitable for the beach or garden. A certain amount of basic equipment is required, but this may easily be acquired.

At each end of a pitch 16 yards long are two wickets, made of hardboard, 1 ft. square, nailed to a post protruding 4 ft. 8 in. from the ground. (See fig. 14.) These official measurements can be altered to suit local conditions. A real stoolball bat is 18 ins. long, but we suggest using a sand spade for the beach, or a rounders stick for the garden. A standard tennis ball would be suitable for unofficial play.

Any even number of players can take part, divided into two teams, but eleven a side is best. One side bats, the other fields.

Just as in Cricket, two batsmen stand, one at each wicket inside a batting crease, while members of the other side elect their wicket-keeper and bowlers and place fieldsmen to best advantage. Boundaries can be marked with sticks in the ground, or by a line in the sand.

There are eight balls in an over, and bowlers must throw the ball under-arm; it must not bounce before it reaches the batsman, otherwise it is declared a 'no-ball'. Batsmen can still hit a 'no-ball' and score runs from it by running to exchange ends with each other (as in Cricket). They cannot be out from a 'no-ball'. Deliveries made outside the batsmen's reach are 'wides' and count as one run against the fielders. If the wicket-keeper fails to collect a ball which the batsman has missed,

this is scored as a 'bye' if the batsmen exchange
ends successfully as in Cricket.

The bowler must try to hit the flat face of the
hardboard wicket to get the batsman out, and
other means of dismissal include: a catch direct
from the bat; if the ball hits the batsman when it
would have hit the wicket; if a batsman hits the
ball twice; and if a batsman is run-out (i.e. is out
of his batting crease when the wicket-keeper
touches the wicket, ball in hand).

The game takes its name from the fact that
cricketers originally defended stools, not wickets,
and used their hands, not a bat, to hit the ball.

If one does not want to go to the trouble of
building hardboard wickets, two chairs will serve
admirably.

French Cricket

The origin of this game is doubtful, but it is
unlikely that any Cricket-loving Englishmen could
have dreamed up this variation in which you need
a cricket bat, but no wicket: the batsmen's legs
are the wicket!

However, this is not dangerous because a soft
ball is used. A cricket bat is not essential, for a
tennis racket, or rounders stick makes a good
substitute.

Any number can play, the more the merrier,
all against all. Players decide who should bat first
and then form a large circle around him. The batsman must stand on one chosen spot with his legs
together, defending them with his bat. Throughout
his innings, he must not move from that spot, even

when someone is bowling to him from behind. In this event, he must reach round with the bat behind his legs and continue to defend them at all costs. He is out when the ball touches him below the knees in front or behind; if he touches the ball twice, or if he is caught straight from the bat by a fielder before the ball touches the ground.

Whoever gets the ball after a hit may bowl (under-arm), or give it to another fielder to bowl; but the ball must be thrown from the spot where it was fielded. The fielder who bowls or catches the batsman takes over the bat.

Runs are not usually scored, but they can be. To score one run the batsman must twirl the bat completely round his body with both hands (keeping his feet quite still). If he is wise, he stops as soon as he sees a fielder about to bowl at him.

Passball

This is a form of Football played without kicking. The only use for the feet is to run as fast as you can.

The playing pitch should be longer than it is wide and it may be of any size according to the space available. The game can be played on any surface. There is no limit to the number of players, but they must be evenly divided into two teams. Eleven a side is best. Each team must then select its own formation of forwards, half-backs, full-backs and goalkeeper.

A goal line is marked and goalposts erected at each end of the pitch, any convenient size though 6 ft. high and 6 ft. wide is recommended. In front of each goal, mark out a semi-circle of at least 10 ft. radius. This is the penalty area.

The aim is to score a goal by throwing the ball past the goalkeeper, between the posts and over the goal-line. Neither team may kick the ball, but it is moved along during play by a series of quick running passes and catches. The ball must not touch the ground: if it does, a throw is awarded to the opponents from that spot.

Tackling and all bodily contact is forbidden. Only the hands may be used to intercept a pass and gain possession of the ball.

Players in possession may take only three paces with the ball before aiming to pass it to a colleague.

The goalkeeper may defend his goal with his hands or body, but must never kick the ball away.

He alone may knock the ball to the ground while making a save, whereupon he must immediately throw the ball upfield. Should any defender, other than the goalkeeper, knock the ball down or drop it inside the marked penalty area, a free throw is awarded to the attacking side. This may be taken from anywhere outside the penalty area.

Should one member of the defending side, including the goalkeeper, send the ball over his own goal line, but outside the goal itself, a long throw is taken by an attacker from the appropriate corner. His team-mates may position themselves anywhere in order to try and receive the throw, but they must not obstruct or impede opponents. There is no 'offside' rule.

For all infringements, a free throw is awarded to the opposing side.

Football Tennis

This lively game is ideal for beach or garden.

A tennis court is marked out measuring 16 yards by 8 yards. Across the centre line (in place of a net) are placed a row of forms, chairs, hurdles or other suitable objects of an equal height.

Players face each other and kick or head a football back and forth across the 'net'. The ball may only touch the ground once between playing and receiving, and in making a return a player may only touch the ball once.

Faults (each of which carries a penalty point) are committed when the ball lands outside the court without being touched by an opponent; if it lands in or on the 'net'; if a player touches it more than once before his opponent touches it.

As in Table Tennis, the first to reach 21 points is the winner. If 20-all results, the game must be continued until one takes a clear two points lead over the other (i.e. 22–20, 25–23 etc.). In this case, from 20-all service alternates point by point.

Service is made from behind the base-line with either a throw or a drop kick. If the served ball should touch the 'net', the service must be retaken. After each fifth point there is a service change.

A doubles game can be played using the same rules. The pairs can pass the ball to each other at will, so long as they do not allow it to drop to the ground at any point. They can also volley the ball directly back. Only the method of service alters. A line should be drawn lengthwise to divide the court in half, and service should always come from

the base-line of the right half into the left half
diagonally opposite. For a service fault, the receiving pair are awarded one point.

Capture

This is best played on a pitch measuring 20
yards by 16 yards, but any variation will do providing there is plenty of room for players to run and
jump about.

Across the pitch draw a halfway line so that you
now have two equal areas of 10 × 16 yards. Then,
4 yards in from each end, and parallel to the half-
way line, mark two further lines to form a total
of four areas, the two inner ones being 16 × 6
yards long, and the two outer ones 16 × 4 yards
long.

The two inner areas are each occupied by
opposing teams of 8 to 10 players who face each
other and spread well out. The two smaller outer
areas are reserved for 'captured' players. Having
decided by the toss of a coin which team will first
have the ball, players proceed to shoot it low
across to their opposing team, trying to hit one of
them. The others, in turn, kick the ball back,
trying to hit their opponents.

Whoever is hit by the ball becomes a prisoner
of the kicking side and must go and stand in the
prison area behind them.

Both teams guard their prisoners so that they
should not get hold of the ball. If a prisoner does
manage to secure the ball, he can shoot it directly
at his guards, and if he hits one, that guard must
go to the opponents' prison area.

A prisoner can only be freed when one of his own side sends him the ball with a high lob which travels over the heads of his guards without their touching it. The prisoner must then be allowed to dribble the ball back to his own playing division, whereupon the game continues.

A reasonable time limit is fifteen minutes, and the team which has captured the most prisoners in this time, wins. At no stage may anyone leave his playing area unless, of course, he is made a prisoner or is released from prison.

The ball must not be touched with the hands, nor kicked too hard. In case of infringement, the offenders must give up one prisoner, or if they have no prisoner they will not be allowed to claim the next man they hit.

'TAG' GAMES FOR CHILDREN

Picking the Flowers

The players form two equal groups. One group are the 'flowers', the other the 'pickers'. A line is marked at each end of the playing ground, behind which is the 'home' of each group.

The 'flowers' choose among themselves to represent a particular flower, perhaps a rose, daffodil or bluebell. Each group then advances from 'home' and stands in line facing each other a few yards apart along the centre of the playing ground.

The 'pickers' then attempt to guess the name of

the flower that has been selected, the group leader calling out flower names. As soon as the name selected by the flower group has been guessed, the 'flowers' try to reach sanctuary in their 'home', the 'pickers' chasing them and tagging as many as possible.

Any 'flower' tagged before reaching 'home' must then become a 'picker' and help to 'pick' the other 'flowers' until none are left.

The Witch's Spell

One player is the 'witch' who sits down or crouches on a mat in the centre of a ring formed by the other players. The circle players walk round the 'witch' singing nursery rhymes.

After a time, the 'witch' very slowly begins to rise and when at full height, suddenly calls: 'Here I come', and at once starts to chase the circle players. As each player is tagged by the 'witch', he is 'frozen' into whatever position and place he finds himself at the time he is tagged. The last person to be touched becomes the 'witch' for the next game. If there is a fairly large number of players it may be stipulated that the 'witch' need touch only a certain number, perhaps four, five or six players, the last of whom becomes the 'witch' in the next game.

Head to Tail Tag

This game may be played in any open space.

Groups are formed, each consisting of five, six or seven children. Each group forms a line in which players hold the waist of the one in front.

The 'head', however, (i.e. the first player) now tries to twist around and tag the tail of the group (i.e. the last player). If he succeeds, places may be changed within the group so that each player has the opportunity of being 'head' and 'tail'.

Jack in the Box

One end of the playing area is marked off, this space being 'home'. Near the opposite end of the playing area, a mat or hoop is placed on which 'Jack' crouches. One player takes the role of 'Jack' and the remainder stand within the 'home' area.

The players then walk around 'Jack' singing, 'Jack in the Box, come out and play, catch us now, or we'll run away.'

Without giving any warning 'Jack' jumps clear of his box and attempts to tag as many players as he can before they reach 'home'. The ones 'tagged' are eliminated and the game continues until one player only remains to be tagged. This player is the winner and 'Jack' for the next round.

Circular Tag Your Number

All the players form a wide circle, hands joined. Players then number off in sections of threes, fours, or fives, depending on the total number taking part.

The leader calls out any number not greater than the number in each section, that is, 1 to 3, 1 to 4, or 1 to 5. All the players of this number then begin to run in a clockwise direction around the outside of the circle, attempting to tag the player with the corresponding number running in front. For example, if there are 16 players in all, this

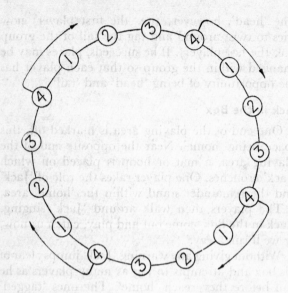

Circular Tag Your Number (Fig. 15)

(being divisible by 4) will produce four players running round the circle each time a number in the range 1 to 4 is called. (See fig. 15).

A competitive element may be introduced by calling each number an equal number of times, after which the individual who made the most tags would be declared the winner.

The Hound and the Rabbits

The playing area is divided by marking out at

one end a space which is to be known as the rabbits' 'burrow'. Near the opposite end a mat, or marked area, stands for the 'bed' of the hound.

When the game starts rabbits and hound are each found within their own territory. The rabbits then come out of their burrow to play by bunny-hopping around the hound. When the hound stirs, each rabbit becomes very alert. When the hound leaves his 'bed', the rabbits scuttle behind him and crouch out of sight.

Eventually the hound picks up their scent and gives chase. Each rabbit scurries off to the burrow before being tagged by the hound. Those tagged remain on the spot as 'dead' rabbits and the game continues until the last rabbit is caught. He or she is the winner and becomes the hound for the next game.

Twin and Triplet

The game begins with two players joining hands and chasing the other players. The first player to be tagged joins with the two original taggers and forms a chain of three. When a second player is tagged, two sets of two players then form up to give chase. The game continues thus until one player only remains to be tagged, and he is the winner.

Hop Tag

In this game, both the chaser and the chased are only allowed to move by hopping. Players may hop on whichever leg they choose, and change from one leg to the other at will.

When not actually being chased, players are allowed to stand on both feet. The person tagged becomes the chaser.

Kangaroo Jump Tag

This is a basic tag game, except that all movements must resemble those of the kangaroo jumping with both feet together and knees slightly bent and so performing a 'spring' jump.

Crab Tag

Again this is the basic tag game, but as the title implies, all movements must be crab-like, that is on all fours (hands and feet) and moving in a sideways direction instead of forwards.

Dog and Rabbit

One child is chosen as a 'rabbit', and a second child as the 'dog'. The remaining players form a double circle, that is a circle in pairs, each player facing inwards.

The 'dog' proceeds to chase the 'rabbit' around the circle. The 'rabbit' may obtain sanctuary by standing in front of or behind any pair in the circle. If the 'rabbit' stands in front of the pair, the rear player becomes the 'rabbit', or if behind the pair, then the front player is the next 'rabbit' to be chased.

Should the 'dog' successfully tag the 'rabbit' before safety is reached, they then reverse rôles, the 'dog' becoming the 'rabbit' and vice versa. To make the game interesting to all, frequent changes are advised, and the children are encouraged to run only short distances.

Interception Tag

The basic tag game is played, but should any player cross, or come between, the chaser and the one being chased, then he or she becomes the one to be chased.

Shadow Tag

This is a game to be played on a bright sunny day when shadows are cast. The object is for the chaser to step on the shadow of a player. When he is successful, the owner of the shadow stepped upon becomes the chaser.

Fox and Hound Tag

Two players are selected, one to be a 'fox', the other a 'hound'. The remaining players form into groups of three and stand at random about the playing ground. Each centre player of a group is a 'fox'; the two outer players are 'hounds'.

The originally selected 'hound' chases the 'fox', who may escape by touching any other 'fox'. The 'fox' touched then becomes the one chased, and his place is taken by the previous 'fox'. The game continues with frequent changes being made to maintain the game's interest.

Should the 'hound' tag the 'fox' before it reaches safety, the tagged 'fox' becomes the 'hound' and the previous 'hound' becomes a 'fox'. At intervals centre players may change places with outer players to give all an opportunity to take an active part in the game.

Fox and Goose Tag

The players form groups, six in each group being best. One player of each group is the 'fox', a second player the 'goose' and the remainder' 'goslings'.

The goose stands with arms stretched out sideways. The goslings form in line behind, each holding the one in front at the waist.

The object now is for each 'fox' to tag the end 'gosling' of his or her group, and for each 'goose' to try to prevent this by moving from side to side. As each player is tagged he drops out of the game. The game continues until all 'goslings' and 'geese' have been tagged.

Bird Snaring

The playing ground should be marked off so that in one corner, a fairly large space serves as a 'forest' or 'wooded glade'. In the corner diagonally opposite, a smaller space is the 'nesting ground'. In a third corner, a space is required as the 'cage'.

All but two players stand in the 'forest'. One of the remaining two players is the 'Mother bird' who stands in the 'nesting' area, and the other player is the 'bird catcher' who takes up a position between the 'forest' and the 'nesting ground'. (See fig. 16).

The object of the game is for each 'bird' to reach the 'nest' without being caught. The 'Mother' calls her family from the forest one by one, each by

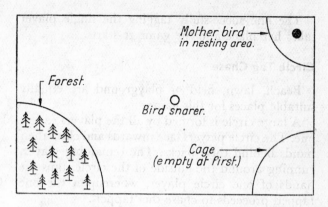

Mother bird in nesting area.

Forest.

O
Bird snarer.

Cage (empty at first.)

Bird Snare (Fig. 16)

name. As each player is called, he or she attempts to cross the area in which the 'bird catcher' stands. If tagged by the 'bird catcher' the player is placed in the cage and must remain there until the end of the game, which is when the last 'bird' is called from the 'forest'.

Statues

A game often played by the girls in the school playground. One child stands at one end of the playing space, and the remaining children stand behind her and at the opposite end. The object is for the children to approach the single player, near enough to tag her without any movement being seen. The single player may turn around and face the other children as often as she wishes. When she does so, they remain perfectly still, as still as 'statues'. If seen to move, they are eliminated.

The one successfully tagging the single player takes her place and the game re-starts.

Circle Tag Chase

Beach, lawn, field or playground are equally suitable places for this game.

A large circle is formed by all the players except one. The circle players face inwards and clasp their hands behind their backs. The remaining player, running around the outside of the circle, taps the hands of one circle player, whereupon the one tapped proceeds to chase the 'tapper'.

The object is for the 'tapper' to try and reach the space left in the circle without being tagged, and for the 'chaser' to try and tag the 'tapper' before he reaches the space.

If a tag is successfully made, the circle player returns to his place and the game continues as before, but should a tag not be made, the circle player then becomes the one to run round the outside of the circle and tap the hands of another player.

The Dodger

This game is played with players in groups of 10 or 12. Each group forms a wide circle with all but 3 of its players. Circle players are spaced at distances of approximately 3 ft. apart.

No. 1 of the 3 remaining players stands within the circle, while Nos. 2 and 3 stand *outside* the circle.

The circle players then number off from 4 upwards. On the signal to start, No. 1 attempts to run round a player or players one, two, or three times, without being tagged by either of the outside players.

Having twice 'encircled' successfully, or on being tagged, the centre player joins the circle. No. 2 becomes the centre player and No. 4 leaves the circle and becomes an outside player.

The game continues until all have played inside and outside the circle. If desired, the number of successful 'dodges' may be counted against the number of successful 'tags' at the end of the game.

Circle Skipping Tag

This is a playground game, or it may be played in an area with definite boundaries such as walls or hedges.

The players form three concentric circles. The extreme inner and outer circles move in a clockwise direction, and the middle circle moves the opposite way. The players link hands and skip round and at the sound of a whistle, or at a call or command, each circle changes direction.

At two blasts on the whistle, or the call 'break', the players disperse, those of the first and second circles running to the boundaries, while the inner circle players attempt to tag them before they are able to reach the walls or hedges.

The Hunter and his Pack

The players stand at one end of the playing area. One player, who is elected to be 'hunter', stands a few yards in front of the others and facing them.

At a given signal, the players attempt to cross the playing space to the home area on the boundary opposite. The 'hunter' tags as many as possible before they reach the other side.

Those tagged become members of the 'hunter's' pack and must assist him in capturing more players by holding them until they can be tagged by the 'hunter' himself. A 'pack' player may only hold one other player at a time, and if a player can successfully drag himself and the 'pack' player into the 'home' area, he is free.

The game continues until all are 'pack' members. Tackling too boisterously should not be allowed.

Relievo

A 'prison' is marked in the shape of a rectangle or semi-circle, the rear boundary of which is formed by a wall or hedge. One player is elected as 'prison guard' and he stands in front of the prison, outside the prison's inner boundary.

Any number of players may take part and, according to the total, one or more players are required to act as 'chasers'. The other players scatter over the playground and, at the signal to start, they try to avoid the 'chasers' and the 'guard' who will attempt to tag them.

Those tagged must go to 'prison' and remain within the 'prison' area. They may only be freed by a player who succeeds in running through the 'prison' without being intercepted.

The guard, who may not enter the 'prison' area, tries to tag any potential rescuer.

Circle March Chase

A large circle is formed by all the players except one who stands in the centre, 20 to 30 yards distant from the circle, a 'home' line is marked.

The centre player selects a number below 40 and calls out the number of his choice. He then proceeds to count aloud, while the circle players march round in step with his counting, until the number selected is reached. At this point players all dash to the safety of the 'home' line, while the centre player attempts to tag a circle player. If successful he changes places with the one tagged.

Net Tag

This is a suitable playground game for any area with well-defined boundaries of walls or hedges. Three players form a 'net', and the remaining players stand along one boundary and attempt to reach the opposite boundary when the 'net' players call 'Run'.

Any player or players caught in the 'net' become a part of it, and the game continues until all are caught. If the 'net' breaks, the player is allowed through.

Mimic Tag

In this game choose a limited field of play, so that players do not become too scattered. Any number can play and the game is the same as basic tag except that each player must mimic the pursuer. If the pursuer skips, all must skip. If he runs dragging one leg, all players do the same.

Time Tag

Any number of players may take part. A time-keeper is required and two teams are formed.

At the signal to start one team scatters, and the others chase. As each player is tagged, he or she must remain standing on the spot. The round is completed when all have been tagged.

The timekeeper notes how long this has taken. The two teams change roles, the pursuers now attempting to tag all the opposing team in less time.

Back-to-Back Tag

A basic game of tag, but this time the one pursued may escape by standing back-to-back with another player, holding his or her arms. A player may only do this when he or she is the player who is being pursued.

Rope Tag

This game is popular with the boys and requires a rope of about 3 yards in length. An ordinary game of tag is played, but the tag must be made with one end of the rope.

Touch Wood

This game is suitable game for campers, picnickers and ramblers playing in the woods. It derives from an old superstition that to touch wood wards off evil spirits, and in this game those who touch wood cannot be tagged. Those who are tagged drop out of the game.

RACES AND RELAYS

Bridge Relay

Teams are formed and each player sits on the ground with legs outstretched. The starting signal is given, whereupon the leader rises and jumps over each pair of legs down the team. He then turns and goes back to his place, hopping over the legs up the team. As soon as he is seated, the next player does the same. The first team to finish wins.

Pick-a-Back or Donkey Relay

Equal teams are formed, and they stand in file behind a line. Approximately 50 ft. away a second line is marked. At the signal to start, the leader transports the second player on his back across the space between the two lines, setting his 'burden' down beyond the opposite line. The second player then returns to the team to carry the third player in a similar manner. The third player brings over the fourth, and so on, until all are behind the second line.

Musical Patterns

If relayed music is not available, the children provide music by singing nursery rhymes or popular songs.

The players form teams of 6 to 8. They then walk about quite freely while the music plays. During this time, the leader calls out a shape, such as a circle, crescent, oval, diamond, oblong, 'Z', 'X', or horseshoe. (See fig. 17).

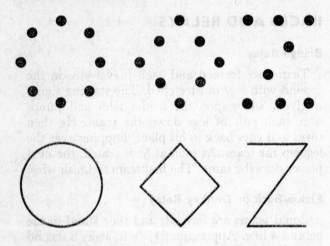

Patterns (Fig. 17)

When the music stops, each team rushes to form the shape called, the first to do so being awarded a point. The team with most points at the end of the game wins.

If music is not being played, a whistle may be blown, or 'Stop' or 'Shape' called out.

Catch and Run Relay

One football or beach ball is required.

Teams are formed, and at the head of each the leader stands facing his team 6 ft. away from the second player. At a distance of approximately 30 ft. from each team an object should be placed or a mark made. At the signal to start, the leader throws the ball to the second player who runs to the mark or object, circles round it and returns to his place. He then throws the ball to the leader and sits down. The third player now receives the ball and does the same. After receiving the ball from the last player, the leader sits at the head of his team. The first team with all its players seated wins.

Dribbling Relay

Competing teams with approximately 6 players in each are formed, and are stationed at intervals of about 20 ft. apart. A ball is required, and various objects are spaced at intervals over a set course. If you are in a field, sticks and stones may be available; on the beach, pebbles or mounds of sand will serve; in a playground, stools, chairs, cartons or wastepaper baskets can be used.

The team stand behind a starting line. At a signal to begin, each player in turn dribbles the ball soccer-fashion along the course around each object to a marked boundary line. On the return, the dribbling may be omitted. The player who is to receive the ball must wait in his place; going out towards the ball is not permissible. The first team to finish, wins.

Craft in a Storm

This is a team game with about 8 players in each team. A team consists of 1 ship, 1 captain, 1 lighthouse, and the remaining players are 'rocks'. (See fig. 18).

'Lighthouses' stand at one end of the playing

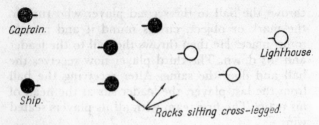

Captain.

Lighthouse.

Ship.

Rocks sitting cross-legged.

Craft in a Storm (Fig. 18).

area and make noises imitating a warning bell or foghorn. The 'ship' and 'captain' are at the opposite boundary, and in between are the 'rocks' sitting crosslegged on the ground, spaced out freely.

The object of the game is for the 'ship' to reach the 'lighthouse' in the shortest possible time. The 'ship' is blindfolded and at the starting signal moves off, with the captain by his side but not touching him.

The 'rocks' whisper 'splash, splash' when the ship is very close to them. If the 'ship' actually touches a 'rock' the captain steers him twice round the rock and puts him on course again. The race is won by the team whose 'ship' is first to reach the 'lighthouse'. This game can be played as a relay, or can be decided by the team with the highest score in a set time.

Leap Frog Relay

This game is particularly popular with boys, but girls also play. Teams are formed and stand in file at one end of the playing ground. The first player of each team moves forward about three paces and makes a 'back' by placing the feet apart and bend-ing to grasp his ankles with his hands. At the signal to start, the second player leaps over the 'back' and then, about three paces from him, makes a second 'back'. This continues along the team until the end player has become a 'back', whereupon the first player then rises and leaps over all the 'backs' and stands to one side. The second player then rises and leaps over the 'backs', after which he stands behind the first player. This continues along the team until all are again standing in file, the first team to do so, winning.

Japanese Sunbonnet

A knotty problem race for girls which is even more fun with boys if you can persuade them to play! A length of ribbon, tape or braid is required. Teams of equal numbers are formed, and stand in file. At the signal to start, the leader faces his team, and ties the ribbon round his head in bonnet-fashion with a bow under the chin. He then claps his hands and the second player unties the ribbon and turns to the third player. The second player ties the ribbon round his head, as the leader has done. This continues along the team until the last player has the ribbon round his head. The game may conclude here, or continue again along the team back to the leader.

Charlie Chaplin Relay

One walking stick or umbrella, one balloon and one small cushion or book are required.

Teams of equal numbers are formed, each standing behind a starting line, beyond which is a

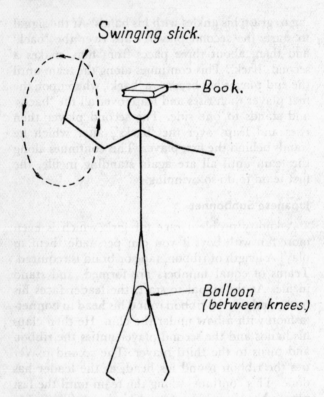

Charlie Chaplin relay (Fig. 19)

course of approximately 7 yards long. A starting 'signal' is given, whereupon each team member in turn is required to cover the course and back, balancing the book on the head, twirling the stick and holding the balloon between his knees. (See fig. 19).

Should either the book or balloon fall from position, it may be replaced, but the player may not proceed until this has been done. The first team to complete the course wins.

Team Obstacle Race

This game is invariably included in the programme at a children's Sports Day. One rope, 2 bean bags, and 2 hoops are required.

A course is set on which the obstacles are laid; the hoops are placed at the beginning and end of the course, and the rope is fixed at a suitable height so that it may be hurdled; the bean bags are each placed in a circle, and these are drawn side by side.

Equal teams are formed, and each stands behind a starting line. At a given signal, the first contestant tries to cover the course, passing a hoop over his head and stepping out of it, jumping over the rope, switching the bean bags from one circle to the other, doing the hoop trick again, and then racing back to his place in the line, whereupon the second player starts off to complete the same course. The winning team is the first one to finish. Many other obstacles may be introduced, depending upon the age and athletic skill of the competitors. Toffee apples on sticks suspended on string are great fun. These must be eaten without being touched by hand. Then there is the object hidden in a basin of flour which must be found by a competitor using only his mouth. This obstacle is guaranteed to produce pasty-faced athletes!

Under and Over Relay

Equal teams are formed. Players spread out in a wide circle, leaving a space of at least 3 ft between each player, and all face in a clockwise direction. Each alternate player stands with legs astride; the others bend to grasp hold of their own ankles, feet apart. At the signal to start the leader travels round the circle, alternately leap-frogging a back and crawling through legs. On returning to his place, he touches off the player in front of him and then he becomes either 'Back' or 'Legs'. The first team to finish is the winner.

MISCELLANEOUS

Children's Competitions

Pussy Wants Your Corner

A lawn, or glade is most suitable for this game. One child is 'Pussy', and the remaining children stand in four groups at each corner of the playing area, or certain points decided upon in the area.

'Pussy' goes from child to child saying 'Pussy wants your corner'. Each time, 'Pussy' is refused, but meanwhile, the children in the other three corners attempt to change places with each other. At the same time, 'Pussy' tries to take the place in a corner before it is reached by the player changing over. On being successful, the corner player misplaced becomes 'Pussy'.

Busy Bee

An uneven number of players are required for

this game. The children pair off and place themselves at random about the playing area. Each pair then carry out the order called by the odd player. Orders could be: 'Link arms', 'Hold hands', 'Stand side by side, each facing the opposite direction', etc.

This continues until 'Busy Bee' is called, whereupon each child must find a fresh partner. The odd player does the same and the one left without a partner must then call the commands for the next game.

River and Road

This game can be played anywhere and any number may take part. One is elected 'leader' and all the remainder stand before the leader and behind a marked line.

The leader has alternative commands to give. He may call (1) River or (2) Road. On the first, all the children are required to jump forward over and beyond the marked line. On the second call, they jump backwards to their original places.

The leader may call 'River' when all are in the river and 'Road' when all are on the road. When calls are made in this way, any one seen to move is eliminated from the game. Suspense can be created by rolling the 'R' which starts both words, so players cannot know which one is to be announced.

Hunt the Slipper

This is popular with younger children, any number of whom may play in any area. A close circle is formed around one player who sits or stands in the centre, holding a slipper, or any object representing a slipper.

The player in the centre gives the slipper to a player in the circle, whereupon the following is chanted: 'Cobbler, cobbler, mend my shoe, have it done by half past two.' The player in the centre tightly closes his eyes and the children chant: 'Cobbler, cobbler, tell me true, which of you has got my shoe?'

During this time the slipper is passed around the circle from player to player behind each back. As the last word of the recitation is spoken, the one holding the slipper at that time keeps it. The centre player is then required to guess who has the slipper, pointing to one whom he thinks is the possessor.

If the guess is correct the centre player changes places with the player in the circle. If incorrect, the game continues as before.

Silent Escape

Two equal teams are formed, the 'escapers' and the 'guards'. The 'guards' scatter over the playing ground and sit or crouch on the ground with eyes tightly closed. The 'escapers' start from one end of the playing ground and silently attempt to reach the opposite end undetected by the 'guards'.

Meanwhile, the 'guards' must be alert for any sound, and if they suspect an escaping player is close, they point in the direction of the sound. If correct, the 'escaper' is eliminated from the game;

if incorrect, one 'escaper' is allowed to reach safety.

After a set time, the teams change over, and at the end the team with the most members in safety is the winner.

Man the Fort

Girls as well as boys participate in this game which can be played anywhere. The children can be organised into teams or compete individually. A leader is required to call out a series of orders to which the players must perform specific actions. Any player who performs incorrectly, or fails to perform, is considered 'lost' and eliminated from the game.

The last player to remain in the game is the winner. If played as a team game the last team to remain wins, or the game may be played for a set time at the end of which the team with most players left wins.

Here are some suggestions for orders:

Eyes Right!—Children look to right.
Eyes Left!—Children look to left.
Attention!—Stand rigidly erect.
Stand at Ease!—Stand feet apart, with hands clasped behind back.
March!—Walking on the spot.
Quick, or Slow March!—Walking on spot quickly or slowly.
Salute!—All children salute leader.
Fire!—Hold imaginary gun and shout 'Bang'.
Fall Out!—All turn round on spot.

Balloon Handball

A balloon is required for this game which may be played in any place free from sharp objects, outside when it is not too windy.

Mark out a pitch approximately 15 yards long and 7 yards wide. Mark goals about 3 yards wide, one in the centre of each end line.

The players form two equal teams and the game starts with the referee tapping the balloon into the air between the two centre players. The object is for each team to score goals by getting the balloon beyond the goalkeeper and into the goal of the opposing side. The following rules should be observed:

(1) The balloon may be handled *only*, with the open hand, not with clenched fists. (2) Holding the balloon is not allowed. (3) To score a goal, the balloon must pass through goal below waist level. (4) Dribbling, by bouncing the balloon on the hand, is permissible. (5) If the balloon goes out of bounds, it is returned to play by the opposite team player, the counterpart to the one who last touched the balloon. (6) After each goal, the game is restarted by the referee tapping the balloon into play at the centre of the field as in the beginning.

Contrary or Opposite

Any ground is suitable for this game in which any number of players can participate, either individually or in teams.

All the players stand before a leader who can be clearly seen. He performs actions and the children are required to repeat these in reverse.

For instance, if the leader bent sideways to the right, the children must bend sideways to the left; or if the leader were to hold his right ear with the left hand, the children hold their left ear with the right hand.

Any mistake or failure to respond means a player is eliminated from the game. The last individual, or remaining team, wins the game. To make the game more competitive, set a time limit, at the end of which the team with the most players remaining is the winner.

Five Stones

This is an ancient game played with a set of five 'stones', which are glazed cubes, 1 in. × 1 in. × 1 in., with four grooved sides. Alternatively, pebbles, or smooth stones, can be used.

Two or more players play, but preferably no more than six in all. Usually, the game is played outdoors by children, perhaps in the playground, but it can also be played indoors, and by adults as well.

Each individual plays in turn until he fails, upon which the next player takes a turn. There are a number of set stages to be performed. On each succeeding round players begin the game from the last stage finished, until someone completes the course.

There are many variations, and players may invent their own course, but the following steps are generally accepted:

(1) All five stones are thrown up and No. 1 must be caught in the palm of the hand. This is

repeated catching 2, then 3, and so on.

(2) As above, but catching the stones on the back of the hand.

(3) The stones are placed on the ground. One stone is thrown up, and while in the air a second stone is picked from the ground as the stone thrown up is caught. This is repeated, picking up 2, 3 and then 4 stones.

(4) The stones are placed in a row on the ground. The first is thrown up and while in the air the second stone is plucked; the first stone is then caught. The first stone is discarded, the second stone tossed and the third plucked and so on.

(5) Stones are placed on the ground. One is thrown up and while in the air two stones are plucked, then the thrown stone caught. This is repeated once, picking up the two remaining stones.

(6) Throw up one stone and pick one stone, then repeat, picking up 3.

(7) Throw up a stone and pick up 4 stones at once.

(8) Throw up a stone, pick up a stone. Retaining both stones, throw up one and replace the other on the ground. Throw up the same stone, this time pick up two. Continue in this manner, throwing up the same stone and increasing the number of stones picked up and replaced until all four are picked up and then returned to the ground.

(9) With the left hand, catch the stone thrown. Continue until 4 stones are within the peri-

meter of the hand.

(10) Throw up one stone pick up a second and catch the first. Throw up 2, pick up a third, catch the two thrown. Continue until all five stones are in the hand.

(11) Throw up 4 stones, pick up the one remaining, catch the four. Throw up 3, place down the two, catch the three. Continue until four stones are on the ground, then throw up the one, and pick up the four finishing with five stones in the hand.

(12) Take all five stones in the hand. Throw up one, place one on the ground, catch the one thrown. Continue one by one, until four stones are on the ground.

With practice one can become very proficient at this game.

Conkers

This ancient and traditional game is still extremely popular in the autumn when horse-chestnuts are in season. Boys collect chestnuts by fair means or foul, but the best kind are those that are allowed to fall themselves when ready to do so. Chestnuts that have been gathered are bored through the centre and baked. After this each is threaded on a separate length of string, knotted at one end. Now for the contest.

Defender and challenger meet in a duel: the defender holds out his conker, suspended at waist level, and his opponent takes his own conker in his left hand, the string tautly grasped in his right. The challenger then takes aim and attempts to strike the suspended conker with his own.

Opponents strike in turn aiming to shatter the rival conker. The successful one may gain special promotion, since a conker is titled according to its number of victories, i.e. a 'oncer', 'twicer', 'thricer', and so on. Should a 'oncer' be victorious over a 'fifther', it becomes a 'sixer'.

Hoop Fight

Hoops are popular with boys and may be of the wooden or plastic variety, or even an old rubber bicycle tyre. Hoops are propelled along on edge, either by the palm of the hand or with a stick.

This particular game is played by 2 players, each with a hoop. The aim is to knock the opponent's hoop off-balance without one's own falling also. This is best achieved at an angle of 45°. It requires much manoeuvring.

Hoola Hoop

A popular craze of recent years which is said to help one slim. A plastic hoop is used. The feet remain firmly on the ground and slightly astride. A circular swaying motion is adopted without lifting the feet from the ground, and the aim is to keep the hoop revolving round the waist. Contests are held to determine who can keep this up the longest or move the hoop fastest.

Aunt Sally

Two or more players may take part, but preferably no more than six. A target is required, and this may be a bottle, can, or similar item which is placed on a boulder, wall, sand-castle, or upturned pail. A ball, balls, rubber quoits or pebbles are thrown at the object from a set distance.

Each player may have three shots at a time. A hit scores a point, and 15 points is game.

Aunt Sally originated in the fair-ground, the target being a clay pipe smoker. For a penny anyone could throw, aiming to knock the pipe from the smoker's mouth.

This game is great fun when played in the snow. Make a snowman to represent Aunt Sally, with a pipe in her mouth and aim to knock the pipe from its place with snowballs.

Hopscotch

One or more players may take part, usually 2 to 6. Hopscotch diagrams (see figures 20–22) are usually chalked on the pavement and a flat stone is tossed so that it will land dead in the centre of the pattern (i.e. not touching any line): if it does not, the player must wait until it is again his turn.

Some common variations are as follows: The first player tosses the stone into box one, using an underhand throw. If the stone lands correctly, the player proceeds from the starting box to box No. 2 by making one single hop on one foot, and then into 3. He then moves to 4 and 5 landing astride, one foot in each box, then hops on one foot to 6, astride in 7 and 8 and then hops on one foot into 9.

The player returns in a similar manner, lifts the stone and returns to the starting box. The stone is then thrown into 2, and the course is covered again, but this time omitting box 2.

This routine continues, a player progressing one number at a time. On completing this sequence the player may initial any box of his choice and then start a fresh sequence, which is as above but this time involves jumping with *both feet* to each number, not hopping.

In boxes with double numbers, each number is taken successively and not simultaneously. On completion, a box is again initialled.

The third sequence consists of walking the course with eyes shut. Succeeding players must avoid all initialled boxes. The stone is flicked into 1, and the player hops into 1. Still hopping, the stone is tapped by the foot into 2. This continues along the course, the player taking as many hops as desired. This is followed by a repetiton of the above, but hopping on the *other* foot.

The fourth sequence is more difficult as the player is limited to one hop only from box to box, plus one hop to direct the stone into the following box. The player and stone are positioned in the starting box. One hop must send the stone into 1, the player following with one single hop. This continues along the course until returned to the starting box.

The next sequence is 'Am I out?' This consists of the player stepping simultaneously into 1 and 6 with eyes shut and when there calling 'Am I out?' If the feet are clearly in the squares she continues similarly into 2 and 5 then 3 and 4. The player must return to the start in similar fashion.

Hopscotch (Figs. 20–22)

The final sequence involves hopping all the way from 1 to 10. One hop drives the stone into 1, the player follows with one hop, and so on to 10. The player tosses the stone into 1 from the start, hops into 1 and then with a hop, drives the stone into 2. The whole course continues in this manner. On returning the stone to the den, it should land clearly in the middle of the square. The player's feet must also be clear of any lines. Landing in the wrong square, and touching the ground with the raised foot when hopping are considered faults.

The diagrams above correspond to the different variations described.

WINTER GAMES

Snowball Battle

Usually snowball fights are spontaneous, but an organised fight is often more fun. Form two equal teams which stand facing each other in two parallel lines. There should be a suitable gap between the two teams and a rear boundary line marked behind each.

'Let battle commence' is called out, and each team member makes and throws snowballs as fast and accurately as he can. Any player retreating beyond the boundary line is out of the game, which ends when one team admits defeat, is called to tea, or runs out of snow or energy!

Snowball Contest

A sport for two players or two teams, each contestant requiring a good supply of snowballs and a shield, which could be constructed from a tin lid.

Contestants stand facing each other at a distance of about 15 ft. apart. At the signal to start they pelt each other with snowballs. If only two players are taking part, they may score the contest by awarding a point for each hit between shoulder and waist level.

Tray Ride

A tray, two sticks with a nail at one end and a plentiful supply of snow are all that are required! The player sits on the tray and propels himself along, pushing himself forward with the sticks, nail-end to the ground. Two or more players may compete to determine who can travel the greatest distance in a given number of 'pushes'.

Giant Snowball Push

Two hard, outsize snowballs are required for this game, each approximately 2 ft. in diameter. A rectangular shaped 'field' is marked out with well-defined end lines. Two teams with 2 to 4 players in each are formed.

The snowballs are placed in the centre of the field a few yards apart. The object of the game is to score points by getting the snowball over the opposing end line, and to hamper the opponents in their efforts.

At the signal to start, each team begins to push its snowball towards the appropriate goal line, frequently dashing back to hamper the opponents. One point is gained each time a snowball crosses the opposing end line.

MARBLE GAMES

Games with marbles are most popular with schoolboys, although adults do play, and nationally famous contests are held annually in Britain. Marbles need not be played outdoors, although the game is often seen on the village green, in the school playground or on a quiet pavement.

Marbles can be rolled, thrown or knuckled. The correct way to shoot a marble is to place it just above the first joint of the thumb, the tip of the thumb being caught by the middle finger and the marble held in place by the first finger. From this position one aims and shoots.

Knuckling is done by placing the back of the hand on the ground, one side of it facing in the direction you wish the marble to travel; the marble is placed on the forefinger and flicked with the thumb.

In Scotland, marbles are called 'bools'. An 'alley' is a small stone or glass marble. The 'taw' is larger, approximately 1 ½ in. in diameter, and usually made of stone.

Alleys

A throwing line is marked, beyond which an alley is placed, at any agreed distance. Marbles are bowled by players, each in turn aiming to hit the alley. The owner of the alley wins all the marbles that miss.

Should a player hit the alley, he takes the owner's place and collects all the marbles that miss. The next successful hit displaces the first winner, and so on until one player has won all the marbles.

Odd and Even

This is a game for two players which is played into a hole in the ground. Each has an agreed number of alleys and contestants toss for the start, the successful one taking all the marbles. He then stands several yards from the hole and tosses the marbles toward the hole.

Should an odd number of alleys settle in the

hole, the thrower claims them and throws again those that remain. If this time an even number are in the hole, the second player is now entitled to throw the marbles.

He likewise claims any odd number of marbles in the hole, losing his turn when an even number are holed. This procedure continues until one player has lost all his marbles.

Five O's

A circle 18 in. in diameter is chalked on the ground, each player placing a marble within. Players shoot in turn, aiming to knock a marble out of the circle. Those successful keep the marble they have hit out.

The first shot is taken from a starting line, but each succeeding turn is taken from the place where the player's marble comes to rest. Should a marble be shot into the circle, it remains there as a target. When the circle no longer contains any marbles, players aim at each other's marbles. Instead of a circle, a square may be marked; one marble is placed in each corner and one in the centre.

Dabblers

Each player contributes a marble and all are placed in a row. Each player in turn shoots at the marbles and claims any which are displaced.

A marble thrown is left lying as a target, and whenever it is hit the owner must add another of his own marbles to the row.

Pyramid

A circle 12 in. in diameter is chalked on the ground. In the centre of the circle one player places 4 alleys in pyramid formation: a base of three alleys with each marble touching the other is constructed, and a fourth is placed on top and in the centre of the three.

The owner of the alleys is allowed to charge the sum of one alley to every player who wishes to aim at the pyramid. Shots are taken in turn from a few yards distant. Should the pyramid be hit, any marbles which roll out of the circle are claimed by the marksman who is also entitled to the return of his original fee.

If a shot is made which comes to rest within the circle, though without hitting the pyramid, the alley is lost to the pyramid owner.

Shoot Your Taw

This is a game making use of alleys and taws, for two players only. Each contributes 6 alleys. A coin is tossed to decide who should start. The winner takes all 12 alleys and throws them all together at a hole in the ground. All alleys holed are won by him. If some alleys remain outside the hole, the second player decides which one the first player must try to hit, whereupon the first player aims and throws his taw at the selected marble. Should a successful throw be made, he can claim all 12 marbles; otherwise he may only claim the ones holed.

The second player then takes his turn by aiming

in a similar manner at the remaining alleys, and
the game continues until one player has won all
12 alleys.

Ring Game

Another game for alleys and taws. A circle approximately 8 ft. in diameter is marked, and into
this each player places, wherever he chooses, an
equal number of alleys.

The players then stand outside the ring and
each in turn rolls his taw, aiming to knock the
alleys out of the ring. Any alleys displaced from
the ring are claimed by the successful marksman.
Should a taw come to rest within the ring, there
it remains as a target and whoever hits it claims
all the alleys won by the taw's owner during that
game.

Spanners

This is a game for two players. One rolls his
marble and when it comes to rest, the second
player tries to hit it with his marble. If successful,
he claims the alley; if not, the first player aims at
the second player's marble. When a hit is made,
the loser must produce another alley.

In a true game of 'spanners' a player claims his
opponent's marble if his own comes to rest close
enough to enable him to flick the two together
with finger and thumb.

Bull in the Ring

Ideal for a grassy lawn or the beach. Players
form a circle, except for one who stands inside it.

Circle players then join hands and on the word 'red', the bull in the ring must try to break out of it by pushing and charging. Once he succeeds, he changes places with the player on the left of where the circle was broken.

DECK GAMES

Deck Quoits

This is an adaptation of the garden game of quoits; but whereas in the garden an iron ring (and often a horse-shoe) is used, ocean travellers seeking amusement on the quarter-deck play with a ring made from rope.

A peg, about eighteen inches high, is set up at a distance of four or five paces from the players, each of whom takes a complete set of quoits and tries to throw them, each in turn, over the peg. Any number of players can take part and, throwing in turn, the first to secure all ten rings (or the most rings) wins.

There are many variations. One, for four players, is to have two pegs arranged some suitable distance apart. Two opponents station themselves at each peg and, using four rings apiece, take it in turn to throw at the far peg. Points are awarded as follows:

1 to the player who has a quoit nearest the peg.
2 to the player who has two quoits nearer than any of his opponent's quoits.
3 to the player with a quoit touching the peg.
4 points for any quoit which rings the peg.

The two players at the other end then pick up the quoits and make their throws, again at the peg furthest from them. They score in the same way and victory goes to the team which first scores 21 points. The 'best of three' is usually played, changing ends after each game.

Target Quoits

Still using the rings made of rope (or those specially made from rubber), here is another game in which accuracy of aim counts most.

At one end of the deck mark out three big circles, numbering them 1, 2 and 3. Two or four players stand at an agreed distance, each with four quoits. The object is to throw the quoits to land in the circles and score points.

Team players throw alternately and may try to dislodge opponents' quoits from the circles. When all players have finished, the final score is counted up. Only those quoits completely within the circles count, and the team with the highest number of points wins.

Bucket Quoits

Place a bucket on the deck and mark out a throwing line: 15 ft. for men, 10 ft. for women and children. Players each throw four quoits, scoring one point for each one which goes directly into the bucket. Twenty-one points makes game.

Shuffleboard

This is a form of Shove ha'penny, but on a giant scale. The scoring board (seen in fig. 23) is marked

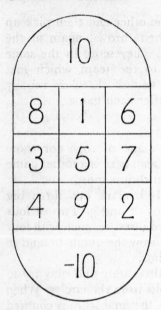

8	1	6
3	5	7
4	9	2

10

−10

Shuffleboard (Fig. 23)

on the deck, and can be of any convenient size, though usually it is about 20 ft. square.

The game, like Bowls, may be played by two or three individuals, or by four taking sides. Using wooden shovel-brooms from behind a starting line (nine or ten paces for women and children, a little farther for men) wooden discs are pushed on to the target board. Discs must come to rest cleanly inside a square to score the appropriate number of points.

Discs which touch any of the lines do not count

and any which lie in the minus-10 enclosure must have that amount deducted from the score.

Fifty-one points must be scored to win a game, and three games make a match. Not only must 51 be scored to win, but that total must not be exceeded. Therefore, if one player (or one team) has a running total of 43, their sole object is to score 8—and no more.

Each player uses six discs, preferably of the same colour for quick recognition by members of a team. Turns are taken alternately, and it is permissible to knock an opponent's disc out of a square and on to a line so that it does not score. Points are reckoned only when all the discs have been played.

An alternative method is for players to stand at either end of the board, about nine paces from the half-circles. If four are playing, a pair of rival players must be together at each end. The game is as before with each player alternately driving his own discs into the target area.

Bullboard

This is a simplified version of Shuffleboard and is played with quoits. A scoreboard (as seen in fig. 24) is drawn up on the deck to an overall measurement of 4 ft. long by 3 ft. wide (i.e. each division being 1 ft. square).

Players each have six quoits and the men stand 10 ft. away, the women 7 ft. Taking turns, they throw all their quoits one by one on to the scoreboard, aiming first for the 1 and then, in correct

BULL	10	BULL
8	1	6
3	5	7
4	9	2

Bullboard (Fig. 24)

sequence, for each number up to 10. The whole quoit must land in a square to count.

Any quoits which land on lines are ignored. Once 10 has been scored, the thrower must try to get the left-hand B (Bull); then the right-hand B (Bull). Next, the whole sequence is reversed, starting with the right-hand Bull, then the left, then 10 all the way down to 1 again.

When a player has thrown all six quoits, he starts his next turn at the point where he finished the first. For example, if after his first six throws he has been successful with numbers 1, 2 and 3, he will next start at 4 and so on.

The first player to work his way from 1 to the right-hand Bull, and then all the way back again, is the winner. A player may try to edge his own wasted discs into other squares and the score will count if he succeeds. But, if at any time, a quoit lands on one of the Bulls out of turn, the player responsible must go back one square. For example: if trying for 10 a player lands on a Bull, he must return to 9 again.

Quoit Tennis

This is one of the most popular quarter-deck games and is played on a court—40 ft. × 9 ft. for singles; 40 ft. × 18 ft. for doubles (See fig. 25).

A rubber quoit is thrown from hand to hand over a 5 ft. high net and, as in most tennis games, there are services, faults and rallies.

The object is to throw a quoit, under-arm and without 'spin' or 'wobble', to an opponent, who must catch it cleanly with one hand and return it immediately, using the same hand for catching and returning.

Unlike Lawn Tennis, but as in Badminton, only the serving side can score points. A point is lost when the quoit touches the ground or goes out of the court, or fails to clear the net, or when a player uses both hands to catch it.

The main rules to observe are:

1. The side which wins the toss chooses ends and serves.
2. Service is begun from the right-hand court

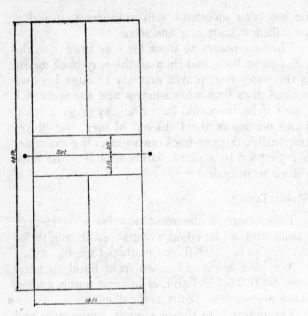

Quoit tennis (Fig. 25)

(thereafter alternately left and right) by throwing the quoit over the net to the opponent standing in the right-hand court diagonally opposite.

3. Only one service is allowed, except when the quoit touches the net in passing over; it is then taken again.

4. Points are only scored by the serving side. Therefore if a fault is made by the server (failing to clear the net or landing outside the receiver's

court) or the server loses a rally, the opponents score no points but win service and so the possibility of scoring in the next rally.

5. A game is won by the player, or side, who first scores fifteen points.

6. After each game, players change ends and the best of three games wins the set and match.

7. In the singles game, the quoit passes across the net from one player to the other. In doubles, partners play and receive 'shots' alternately.

8. There is a three feet 'dead ball line' on either side of the net and the quoit must not drop into this area; if it does a point is lost. Neither must players stand inside this 'neutral' area. (They lose a point if they do).

9. Points are also lost when the quoit hits the ground; is touched by both hands; is thrown over-arm; is 'spun' or 'wobbled' in the air, or is held by one hand while a step is taken.

The whole aim of the game is to keep the quoit moving quickly back and fro without any delay, returning it in such a way as to 'wrong-foot' your opponent.

There are almost as many different names for Quoit Tennis as there are rules (Ring Tennis, Deck Tennis, Ship Tennis and Tenikoit). Many people elect to make up their own rules, which can be based either on Lawn Tennis or Badminton.

Acknowledgments

The publishers and editor would like to thank the following for permission to reproduce photographs: J. Allan Cash, the British Travel and Holidays Association, Central Press Photos, Fox Photos, Mirrorpic, Mustograph, Henry Grant, David Moore, Peter Waugh, the Keystone Agency and the Orient Line.

INDEX